California Bar Examination

Performance Tests and Selected Answers

July 2014

The State Bar Of California
Committee of Bar Examiners/Office of Admissions

180 Howard Street • San Francisco, CA 94105-1639 • (415) 538-2300
845 S. Figueroa Street • Los Angeles, CA 90017-2515 • (213) 765-1500

PERFORMANCE TESTS AND SELECTED ANSWERS

JULY 2014

CALIFORNIA BAR EXAMINATION

This publication contains two performance tests from the July 2014 California Bar Examination and two selected answers for each test.

The answers were assigned high grades and were written by applicants who passed the examination after one read. The answers were produced as submitted by the applicant, except that minor corrections in spelling and punctuation were made for ease in reading. They are reproduced here with the consent of the authors.

CONTENTS

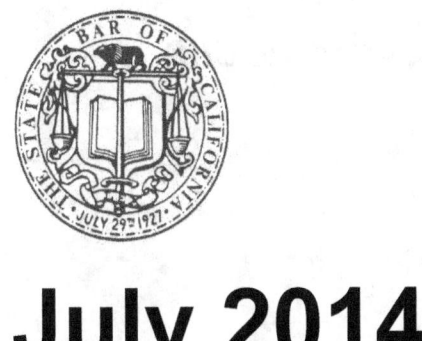

July 2014

California Bar Examination

Performance Test A

INSTRUCTIONS AND FILE

TEHAMA COUNTY V. TEPEE CAMPGROUND

TEHAMA COUNTY V. TEPEE CAMPGROUND

INSTRUCTIONS

1. This performance test is designed to evaluate your ability to handle a select number of legal authorities in the context of a factual problem involving a client.

2. The problem is set in the fictional State of Columbia, one of the United States.

3. You will have two sets of materials with which to work: a File and a Library.

4. The File contains factual materials about your case. The first document is a memorandum containing the instructions for the tasks you are to complete.

5. The Library contains the legal authorities needed to complete the tasks. The case reports may be real, modified, or written solely for the purpose of this performance test. If the cases appear familiar to you, do not assume that they are precisely the same as you have read before. Read each thoroughly, as if it were new to you. You should assume that cases were decided in the jurisdictions and on the dates shown. In citing cases from the Library, you may use abbreviations and omit page citations.

6. You should concentrate on the materials provided, but you should also bring to bear on the problem your general knowledge of the law. What you have learned in law school and elsewhere provides the general background for analyzing the problem; the File and Library provide the specific materials with which you must work.

7. Although there are no restrictions on how you apportion your time, you should probably allocate at least 90 minutes to reading and organizing before you begin preparing your response.

8. Your response will be graded on its compliance with instructions and on its content, thoroughness, and organization.

APEL & ESTEPE

Attorneys at Law

MEMORANDUM

TO: Applicant

FROM: Lou Estepe

SUBJECT: Tehama County v. Tepee Campground

DATE: July 29, 2014

We represent Jane Maya, who owns and operates Tepee Campground. Jane was served with a Notice to Abate by the County Attorney's Office of Tehama County. We have an abatement hearing scheduled. The abatement hearing is a trial before an independent administrative law judge.

Before I write my brief, please draft an objective memorandum that discusses and analyzes the charges made in the Notice to Abate, and evaluates our chances of prevailing against each charge. Take into consideration arguments likely to be made by the County. A separate statement of facts is not necessary. Instead, use the facts in your analysis of the charges.

TEHAMA COUNTY, COLUMBIA

Al Read
County Attorney
P.O. Box 1000
200 King Street
Short Mill, Columbia

June 13, 2014

Jane Maya
Tepee Campground
78200 West Bank Road
Tehama County, Columbia

NOTICE TO ABATE

Property Address:

Recreational Park Trailers at Tepee Campground
78200 West Bank Road
Tehama County, Columbia

NOTICE IS HEREBY GIVEN that the following conditions, activities, or uses exist at Tepee Campground, 78200 West Bank Road, Tehama County, Columbia, in violation of the following Tehama County Land Development Regulations (LDRs): 54 recreational park trailers (RPTs) present in a district zoned rural/residential.

1.   The RPTs are permanent structures in violation of LDR, Section 222.1; and

2.   The RPTs are an enlargement, expansion, or material increase in intensity of a nonconforming use; or a change to another nonconforming use that is not a materially less intense use -- in violation of LDR, Sections 541.1, 541.2, and 541.3.

Required Corrective Action: Removal of all RPTs within 10 days of receipt of this Notice, or by June 30, 2014, whichever date is later.

Please comply promptly with this Notice or I will refer the matter for an immediate abatement hearing.

Sincerely,

Al Read

County Attorney, Tehama County

NEWSPAPER ARTICLE

North Country Boomerang

June 19, 2014

GLAMPING DEBUTS ON WEST BANK ROAD

Jane Maya Rolls in 54 Recreational Park Trailers to Provide a Glamorous Camping Experience.

by Damon Suarez, Boomerang Reporter

Last Monday, a red GMC Denali towing a white recreational trailer rolled down the Tepee Campground drive toward the rental office, past a row of new modern wood-paneled cabins.

The sport utility vehicle was pushed down in the back by the weight of the trailer. Jane Maya, owner of Tepee Campground, guessed the SUV and trailer measured about 55 feet, still shy of the campsite's limit of 78 feet for recreational vehicles (RVs).

"That's not even as big as the biggest RV trailers," she said, noting the Denali and trailer didn't compare to the mega land yachts that come to her campground on West Bank Road.

After parking, the owner turned on a gas-powered generator to run his air conditioner and appliances. The loud hum was expected to reverberate throughout the campground until his departure.

In contrast, Maya's new mobile "cabins" -- which are called recreational park trailers or RPTs -- took up just 39 feet of each RV slot on which they sat. They too are on wheels, and were towed by light-duty pickup trucks. But with electricity already hooked up, there were no noisy generators needed.

Guests at some of the new cabins sat on the front porch, sipping soda.

"This is so much more subdued and quiet, like being in the outdoors was meant to be," Maya said of the cabins, which she trucked in last week. "But it's the same use."

With the arrival of the mobile cabins, Maya estimates the number of guests such as those driving the big diesel Denali and trailer will decrease by hundreds. In doing so, she will transition her decades-old Tepee Campground to a resort called "Solitude." She said Solitude Resort will be a new "glampground" where guests can still camp under the stars, albeit in a mobile cabin with creature comforts -- running water, high-definition TV, and feathered pillows.

"This is the evolution of camping," she said. "Glamping is in between staying in a hotel and camping. It's glamorous camping."

With diesel prices at more than $4 a gallon, it's no wonder that occupancy of these cabins is nearly full every night and rentals on her RV slots are down about 40 percent. "I don't think we'd stay open another 5 years just renting to RVs and tent campers," she said. "But with recreational park trailers, we expect full occupancy year-round."

Campgrounds across the country are parking these units on-site, according to Maya. "It's the future for campgrounds," said Maya. She added, "And we go from gas guzzling motor homes to families who arrive in hybrids or public transportation to stay in certified green trailers."

Maya said that she will only accept short-term rental, no permanent or long-time tenants, but does expect to rent the trailers year-round. "We always have," she said.

Maya's trailers are 12-feet wide, built on a chassis, 39-feet long and measure about 395 square feet. "Everything is built onto the trailer," said Maya. "I personally made sure that they fit the federal government's definition of an RV." Maya added, "No sheds or decks attached, like you see at mobile home parks."

Maya's cabins are paneled with reclaimed mountain snow fencing and each comes with a fireplace, hardwood floors, and wireless internet. Outside, guests have a deck with a grill and a private outdoor campfire lawn.

In the kitchen, guests will find a stove, refrigerator, microwave oven, and dishwasher. Bathrooms come with a sink, granite countertops, and large stand-up shower.

The queen-size plush-top mattresses are covered with luxury linens, goose down pillows, and European-style bed covers. Furniture and all-wood fixtures were built from pine-beetle-killed trees.

Maya charges $175 to $300 a night to rent one of her glampers.

NEWSPAPER ARTICLE

Tehama Times Eagle

June 24, 2014

TEPEE CAMPGROUND GOING ROGUE?

It's an RV, It's a Cabin, It's a Modular Home.

by Zena Owens, Times Eagle Correspondent

Though enmeshed in a legal battle with Tehama County about whether she needs permission to use cabins-on-wheels, Jane Maya, owner of Tepee Campground, decided to bring the units in anyway. She believes they are allowed, while the County Planning Department says she needs a special permit for them.

Recreational park trailers, or RPTs as they are known in the trade, are a fast-growing trend in the camping community. They bear little resemblance to a typical RV. They look more like modular cabins.

"Jane says these RPTs are just like RVs. I don't agree," said Planning Director Jason Drulard.

County land regulations do not allow permanent structures in campgrounds without the permission of the County. Two months ago, Maya sought permission to bring RPTs on 54 of her RV sites.

Drulard acknowledged that Maya at first tried to work with the County. "I really regret what has happened," Drulard said. "We persuaded Jane to seek a conditional use permit, but then her neighbors flooded the County Commissioners with complaints, and they temporarily suspended the process."

Drulard admits that government does not move at the pace of commerce, but says he is just following protocol. "I am absolutely appreciative of her frustration right now," Drulard added.

Drulard pleaded with Maya to hang in there. "She's come so close with this application. To bail now, it's a shame," Drulard said. "But at this point, given that she has withdrawn her application for a conditional use permit, we can't just let her bring the units in."

The delay was the last straw for Maya. "I was at the end of my rope," she said.

"I had them built, ready for delivery, and even booked, when the County Commissioners decided not to hear my case," Maya exclaimed.

Maya is moving RPTs onto her site as quickly as they can build them in Red Bluff. Maya herself designed the cabins with a builder of prefabricated modular homes.

"Just because I made these cool, I shouldn't be persecuted for that," Maya said. "If they looked tacky, I would probably have gotten approval."

Everything Maya wants to do hinges on the County's definition of an RPT.

"The Planning Department and the County Commission never got to decide whether an RPT is a structure. Now a judge will do it," lamented Drulard. If the units are in violation, fines and legal action could result.

What will Maya do if she loses?

"If they want to defeat this project, then they are going to have the Wild West out here," Maya warned. "We can pack this place with aluminum-sided trailers. I can rent these sites for $600 a month and fill every one. It's going to be filled with people rebuilding their dirt bikes out front. So if they want to see that, game on."

CONDITIONAL USE PERMIT APPLICATION
STAFF REPORT

BY JASON DRULARD, PLANNING DIRECTOR, TEHAMA COUNTY

April 30, 2014

APPLICANT: Tepee Campground

OWNER: Jane Maya

REQUEST: Conditional Use Permit to use Recreational Park Trailers (RPTs) on 50% of the current campsites, to be located on the site year-round and rented for visitor use on a short-term basis.

PLANNING DEPARTMENT STAFF FINDINGS:

PROJECT HISTORY

Tepee Campground has been in existence since the mid-1970s. Thereafter, when the County adopted its first land use regulations, the campground was a permitted nonconforming or a "grandfathered" use.

In 1994, the current Tehama County Land Development Regulations (LDRs) were adopted and all properties within Tehama County were rezoned. As part of that rezone, the Tepee Campground property was located in a district zoned rural/residential. Within the rural/residential zoning district, campgrounds are a permitted use requiring a Conditional Use Permit (CUP). Since this was a campground that existed prior to the current zoning regulations and would require a CUP under the current LDRs if newly proposed, the existing campground is considered a permitted nonconforming use per the definition of Nonconforming Use (LDR, Section 540).

In 1979, the campground had a total of 142 campsites (33 tent sites and 109 RV, i.e., recreational vehicle, sites) on 7.6 acres, and structures (A-frame office, residential duplex, shed and store) totaling 5,100 square feet. Under current permitted density ratios for campsites, Tepee Campground would have the same number of sites as it has now.

The current site consist of 33 tent sites, 109 RV sites, and related structures.

<u>ISSUES</u>

<u>Issue 1</u>:   Are RPTs recreational vehicles (RVs) or are they structures being used as lodging?

Recreational park trailer (RPT) use is not defined in the LDRs generally or in the campground definition. The LDRs, when written, could not have contemplated all uses or inventions. Campgrounds are defined in the LDRs as "establishments providing overnight or short-term sites for recreational vehicles, trailers, campers or tents, that have no permanent structures. . . . " LDR, Section 222.1.

Classification depends on whether RPTs are considered recreational vehicles (RVs) or structures. The County Building Department has not treated RPTs, or RVs, as buildings in the past. (See attached Building Department Memorandum.)

RVs, in general, are defined in, although not regulated by, federal regulations (24 C.F.R. Section 3282.8 (g)). The RPT industry claims that RPTs fit within the criteria of RVs. The RPT industry has established construction standards for RPTs. To meet the standards, RPTs must be limited to 400 square feet, built on a single chassis, mounted on wheels, and must comply with various requirements for electrical, plumbing, and heating systems. If certified under the RPT industry standards, many states treat RPTs as vehicles; for example, by taxing them as vehicles. (See attached Recreational Park Trailer Industry Association letter.)

Although RPTs are hauled to their ultimate resting place on wheels, they hook up to sewer systems, draw power from the grid, and feature running water and refrigeration.

If classified as structures, RPTs could not be placed in a campground (LDR, Section 222.1); they would require building permits and would be subject to the County Building Code requirements for buildings. Neither short-term rentals of lodging, nor mobile home parks, which are intended for long-term occupancy, would be permitted in a rural/residential zone without a conditional use permit.

Issue 2:   Are RPTs an enlargement, expansion, or material increase in intensity of a nonconforming use, or a change to another nonconforming use?

This change is not a new development in a rural/residential zone, but rather it is a change in the operational characteristics of what exists on the property. The overall proposed development, as an existing nonconforming use, may not be compatible with the surrounding uses (a campground among rural residences).

The applicant describes the use as a form of campground use, and thus identical to the existing non-conforming use. The fact that customers stay for short periods of time, that the vehicles may meet the federal definition of recreational vehicles (RVs), and that the owner intends no expansion of the existing pads lends support to this view.

By affixing the so-called trailers to her land and attaching them to services, however, has the applicant changed the use of her property? No longer is she charging visitors $27.50 per night to park vehicles in a campsite. Instead, she will be charging more than $175 per night for a room.

Staff notes significant differences between campgrounds and a property equipped with RPTs. In the former, the patron brings a vehicle to the property and removes it when leaving. In the latter, the landowner maintains the vehicle on the property, rents it to a patron and repairs, maintains, and cleans it between occupancies. The use may be very similar to a motel unit in that a guest comes to the campground in a passenger vehicle, stays a limited time, leaves, and the campground staff cleans the unit to prepare it for the next guest. As noted above, short-term rentals, such as a motel or hotel, would not be permitted in the rural/residential district.

A common complaint from neighbors is that the campground has expanded the number of sites over time, and that the introduction of RPTs will further increase site density. Staff cannot substantiate either claim. The County's historical aerial photography indicates that the campground's current configuration is almost identical to the 1978 layout, suggesting little, if any, expansion has occurred over the years in terms of site development. This application seeks to replace one-half of the current RV sites with RPT sites. There would be no increase in the number of sites.

RPTs will be no bigger than many, if not most, RVs. The maximum length of RPTs is 40 feet, although they may be wider, at 12 feet versus 8 feet for most RVs. In general, the footprint or structure floor area of the pads will be smaller than the current pads. The bulk of current RVs, in total, may be greater than proposed RPTs.

Some neighbors and nearby businesses have supported the appearance of the attractive wood-sided RPTs and the enhanced landscaping.

The County Transportation Department estimates a slight reduction in traffic entering and leaving the campground, more importantly, replacing the less nimble fuel-inefficient RVs with passenger cars. The Traffic Impact Assessment is attached.

Applicant also asserts other benefits mitigating or minimizing potential adverse impacts to neighboring properties, such as benefits to air quality and fuel consumption. (See attached Air Quality & Fuel Consumption Analysis submitted by the applicant.)

The campground is one block from a county bus shelter, and across from the extensive network of pathways for hiking and biking. The site has safe, convenient, and direct access to public transportation.

From comments and community complaints, it is probable that there has been a small amount of long-term use on the property for many years. Long-term use would be an established, historical use. Applicant could probably convert part or all of the campground into a mobile home park.

Applicant has proposed a 30-day stay limit for the entire campground -- all RPTs, RVs, and tent campers. Current uses by long-term renters would go away. If the CUP is granted, staff recommends that it be limited so that only short-term rentals are allowed at the campground, not only for RPTs, but for all users. Precluding continuation of long-term use at this campground, located as it is in the rural/residential zone, has significant benefit for the character of the surrounding neighborhood, by preventing RPTs from becoming in effect a mobile home park.

MEMORANDUM

TO: County Commissioners

FROM: Director, Building Department

DATE: April 21, 2014

RE: Recreational Park Trailers

The Tehama County Building Code has no provisions on recreational park trailers (RPTs) or any other recreational vehicles (RVs). We have never issued a building permit for one, nor inspected an RPT before or after installation.

The Building Code does not make a distinction between types of RVs, whether fifth wheels, towable trailers, or motor homes; it considers them all to be RVs. While the building code recognizes RVs, it does not regulate them.

I checked with Peter Mendez of the HUD Office on Manufactured Housing, and he said that RPTs are not being regulated by HUD.

If the Commissioners decide that RPTs are structures, then of course the full Building Code regime of permits for construction, code standards, and inspection would be applicable.

In the opinion of the Tehama County Building Department, RPTs pose less of a risk to the public than a conventional RV and therefore should not be subject to anything that we are not willing to require of fifth wheels, towable trailers or motor homes, provided the property was located in an area zoned for such use.

RECREATIONAL PARK TRAILER INDUSTRY ASSOCIATION, INC.

Washington, D.C.

recreationalparktrailers.com

April 15, 2014

Dear Commissioners:

The Recreational Park Trailer Industry Association (RPTIA) is the national trade association representing the manufacturers of recreational vehicle park trailers and their related suppliers. The Association also represents allied retailers, RV parks and resorts.

We submit this letter in support of the application from Tepee Campground for a conditional use permit.

Recreational park trailers (RPTs) are RVs primarily designed as temporary living quarters for recreation, camping or seasonal use. They are built on a single chassis, mounted on wheels, and have a gross trailer area not exceeding 400 square feet in the set-up mode. One type is less than 8'6" in width and designed for frequent travel on highways, while the other and more popular type is usually 12' in width, must be transported with special movement permits from state highway departments, and are usually sited in a resort or RV park for an extended term, typically several years.

A determination by your county that these vehicles are "structures" would have a catastrophic impact on the campground industry and businesses related thereto. All RVs in the United States have been classified by the states and federal government using the criteria outlined above. If Tehama County were able to classify one of these RV units as a "structure" and require it to meet local building codes as a "structure," this same logic could then be applied to all other RVs, including folding camping trailers, travel trailers, fifth wheel travel trailers, and motor homes. Local building codes are designed for structures that are rigid, not for vehicles that are designed for transport on roads and highways. While the RPT might look like a building, it is not. It is a vehicle.

Respectfully submitted,

George Rubottom
Executive Director

TRAFFIC IMPACT ASSESSMENT

TEPEE CAMPGROUND

For TEHAMA COUNTY PLANNING DEPARTMENT

By Lopez-Granada Engineering

Big City, Columbia

April 21, 2014

Summary:

This traffic impact assessment is a narrowly focused examination of a proposed change to the operational characteristics on the existing recreational vehicle site. While RVs would still visit the site, one-half of the use would shift to patrons coming in SUVs and passenger cars. The proposed development will slightly reduce vehicle traffic flow on West Bank Road, introduce no increase in traffic impacts, and provide more than adequate vehicular site access. The change would have the benefit of replacing the less nimble fuel-inefficient RVs with passenger cars. The applicant's proposal would likely increase the number of patrons, yet decrease the number of recreational vehicles accessing and exiting the property.

AIR QUALITY & FUEL CONSUMPTION ANALYSIS FOR RECREATIONAL VEHICLE SITE REPLACEMENT WITH RECREATIONAL PARK TRAILERS

Report prepared for Tepee Campground

By Science for Hire

April 10, 2014

ABSTRACT

Tepee Campground is seeking to diversify a portion of its inventory to include recreational park trailers (RPTs) on premises. By swapping out a subset of existing recreational vehicle (RV) spaces for RPT sites, the Campground will be positioned to offer visitors an ecologically friendly alternative to driving or towing their lodging, which is inherent to RV travel.

Our study has shown that replacing one traditional RV site with one RPT site could save approximately 9,500 gallons of fuel and reduce the CO_2 emissions released into the atmosphere by 363,000 pounds each year. If Tepee Campground replaced 54 RV sites with RPT sites, it would save 513,000 gallons of fuel consumption and reduce carbon emissions by 19,602,000 pounds or 9,801 tons annually.

July 2014

California
Bar
Examination

Performance Test A

LIBRARY

TEHAMA COUNTY v. TEPEE CAMPGROUND

<u>LIBRARY</u>

SELECTED TEHAMA COUNTY
LAND DEVELOPMENT REGULATIONS

DIVISION 200: ZONING DISTRICT REGULATIONS

The purpose of this article is to establish zoning districts and uses that regulate the type and density of land uses within the county to:

A.   Ensure the protection of the desired community character of each zoning district;

B.   Promote adequate housing and business activity within the county;

C.   Promote stability of existing land uses and protect them from inharmonious influences and harmful intrusions; and

D.   Ensure that uses and structures enhance their sites and are compatible with the natural beauty of the county's setting and critical natural resources.

DIVISION 220: ZONING DISTRICTS USES

* * * * *

Section 222.   Campgrounds

222.1.   Campground use means establishments providing overnight or short-term sites for recreational vehicles, trailers, campers or tents, that have no permanent structures other than a management office, laundry, small grocery, storage facility, and sanitary facilities that shall be solely for the occupants of the campground.

222.2.   Camping Sites. Each camping site in the campground shall consist of a camp pad that provides adequate parking, the camp site (including a fireplace or barbecue, and a table), a pole for hanging food stores or bear proof boxes, where appropriate, and a surrounding active recreational area.

* * * * *

Section 540.   Nonconforming Use

Nonconforming use means any use of land, building or structure which was established pursuant to the zoning and building laws in effect at the time of its development, but which use is not permitted by these Land Development Regulations for the zoning district in which it is located. A use permitted by right at the time of its development, but now designated as a nonconforming use for the zoning district in which it is located, is a permitted nonconforming use. A Conditional Use Permit is not required to continue the existing use, but a Conditional Use Permit is required for any change of use.

Section 541.   Change in Use or Characteristics

541.1.   A nonconforming use shall not be enlarged or expanded in areas of structure or land occupied.

541.2.   A nonconforming use shall not be materially increased in intensity.

541.3.   A nonconforming use shall not be changed to another nonconforming use unless any new use is a materially less intense nonconforming use.

541.4.   The determination of the level of intensity shall include consideration of traffic generated, perceived level of activity, operational characteristics and potentially adverse impacts on neighboring lands.

TALL TIMBERS RESORT V. OREGON CONSTRUCTION DEPARTMENT
Appellate Division (2010)

On November 30, 2008, the Commissioner of the State of Oregon Construction Department (Commissioner or Department) adopted a new set of regulations, which determined that recreational park trailers (RPTs) are subject to the State Uniform Construction Code (Construction Code).

Appellants, who are a seller of RPTs, the owner of a campground in which RPTs are installed, and the owners of an RPT, challenge the validity of these regulations on the ground the Construction Code Act does not confer authority upon the Department to regulate RPTs under the Construction Code.

The applicable administrative regulation defines a "recreational park trailer" (RPT) as a trailer-type unit that is primarily designed to provide temporary living quarters for recreational, camping, or seasonal use, that meets the following criteria:

1. Is built on a single chassis mounted on wheels;

2. Has a gross trailer area not exceeding 400 square feet in setup mode, and, if less than 320 square feet in the setup mode, would require a special movement permit for highway transit; and

3. Is certified by the manufacturer as complying with standards set by the recreational park industry.

In proposing the adoption of the challenged regulation, the Department stated:

Commonly referred to as "park models," recreational park trailers (RPTs) are types of recreational vehicles (RVs) that are installed in recreational vehicle parks or condominium campgrounds based upon long-term ground leases, or ownership in the case of condominium campgrounds. Site built appurtenances such as decks, sunrooms, and others are often attached to the recreational park trailers. They are typically used as vacation homes.

RPTs are constructed in generally the same manner as single family dwellings and incorporate the same types of electrical, plumbing, and mechanical systems as dwellings.

An RPT is closed construction, which means that it arrives at the site already assembled so that most building, plumbing, mechanical and electrical systems cannot be inspected because they are already concealed.

RPTs may be found sited in campgrounds, in mobile home or manufactured home parks or on individual lots. Wherever they are and whether they are used for vacation purposes or as permanent residences, they are subject to the requirements of the Construction Code.

The Department received extensive comments regarding its proposals for adoption of the regulation. Those comments and the Department's responses mirror to a substantial extent the arguments presented in this appeal.

The purposes of the Oregon Construction Code Act include "providing requirements for construction and construction materials consistent with nationally recognized standards" and "insuring adequate maintenance of buildings and structures throughout the State and adequately protecting the health, safety and welfare of the people." To accomplish the legislative objective of protecting the health, safety, and welfare of occupants of buildings and structures, the Legislature delegated authority to the Commissioner of the Department to "adopt a State Construction Code for the purpose of regulating the structural design, construction, maintenance and use of buildings or structures to be erected, and the alteration, renovation, rehabilitation, repair, maintenance, removal or demolition of buildings or structures already erected."

Our Supreme Court has indicated that the Construction Code Act is remedial in nature, and designed to address directly matters affecting health, safety and welfare. By its own terms, the Construction Code Act's provisions must receive liberal construction to advance its purposes.

The key terms of the Construction Code that the Legislature authorized the Department to adopt are "structure" and "building." The Commissioner of the

Department has interpreted "structure" and "building" to include RPTs. The Commissioner cited various reasons supporting this interpretation, including:

- A recreational park trailer (RPT) is a combination of the same types of materials used in any home and it involves all the same safety issues as a home.

- It is intended for the same type of occupancy as any other vacation home.

- A recreational park trailer (RPT) is a structure that is enclosed with exterior walls -- walls identical in construction to those of any dwelling.

- It is clearly designed for housing or shelter and it is arranged for the support of individuals.

- It is equipped with plumbing, electrical and mechanical systems just as is any dwelling.

Appellants challenge the Commissioner's interpretation that RPTs are "structures," arguing that they should be classified as recreational vehicles (RVs). Appellants rely on the definition of RVs contained in the regulations of the Federal Manufactured Home Construction & Safety Standards Act. The Act governs "manufactured homes." The regulations issued pursuant to the Act expressly exclude "recreational vehicles" from the category of "manufactured homes." In the federal regulations, "recreational vehicles" are defined as: (1) built on a single chassis; (2) 400 square feet or less when measured at the largest horizontal projection; (3) self-propelled or permanently towable by a light duty truck; and (4) designed primarily not for use as a permanent dwelling, but as temporary living quarters for recreational, camping, travel, or seasonal use. 24 CFR, Section 3282.8(g).

Appellants contend that RPTs fit the federal definition of an RV. An RPT, however, can be distinguished from a conventional RV. It is a special type of RV that is intended for installation in a "park." They are built under a different standard than conventional RVs. The principal difference between the national consensus standard for RVs and the standards for RPTs, is that the RPT standard covers all types of the requirements typically found in a building code while the RV standard does not.

Appellants cite other distinctions between RPTs and manufactured homes, or most other homes, to support their contention that RPTs are not structures. In their view, both a manufactured or other home is a structure because it is constructed, erected, or attached to something with *a fixed location on the ground*. For example, RPTs have a fifth wheel for hauling and are designed for greater mobility and movement than a manufactured home. An RPT is not manufactured to HUD specifications for a manufactured home and has a maximum area of 400 square feet. The wheels are not removed from the chassis of an RPT, as are wheels from a manufactured home, and an RPT is not placed on a permanent foundation. An RPT is left on its wheels and parked on a recreational vehicle pad. RPTs remain readily movable.

The federal definition of RVs also contains a standard that is entirely dependent upon its intended use, i.e., "designed primarily not for use as a permanent dwelling, but as temporary living quarters for recreational, camping, travel, or seasonal use." 24 C.F.R, Section 3282.8(g)(4). Appellants say the standard is an objective one, and that a reasonably prudent person would use as a temporary dwelling what was designed for temporary use, although such temporary dwelling also may be used for permanent living quarters for one or more families or individuals. Appellants contend that the objective design of the trailer for normal use controls, rather than the subjective *intent* of the user. Thus, travel and recreational design determines the temporary nature of the trailer, notwithstanding that there may be those individuals who may use it as a permanent dwelling.

However, the appellants' contentions, whether they are correct or not, miss the point. We do not need to classify RPTs as either manufactured homes or RVs. The Department has determined that RPTs are structures, even if primarily designed to provide temporary living quarters for recreational, camping, or seasonal use.

The Department's determination that RPTs fall within the Construction Code's definition of "structure" is not plainly unreasonable and therefore must be upheld.

Affirmed.

COUNTY OF LOS BANOS V. LESKIEWICZ

Columbia Court of Appeal (2000)

The County of Los Banos (County) commenced an abatement proceeding to enjoin the defendant-landowners from renting space for recreational vehicles and other camping trailers to members of the public. Defendants own a 14-acre tract of land in Los Banos County, made up of three separate parcels. It is located in a rural-agricultural district, which does not permit the uses made by Defendants of renting camping sites.

Prior to the adoption of the county zoning ordinance, Defendants had improved the 14-acre tract by trimming trees, removing and burning brush, grading, erecting retaining walls, building a road, installing a cesspool, and erecting an outhouse. They also built two tents, a picnic area, and a camping trailer; the trailer was there for about three weeks. During the time, Defendants rented the facilities to the public for camping. For one or two years, the "picnic area-campground" operated in summers to permit outdoor visits for two to four families at a time.

Thereafter, the County adopted its zoning ordinance which did not permit commercial uses, such as campgrounds, in the rural-agricultural district.

Over several years, Defendants erected a building to provide sanitation services for picnickers and campers. The record does not indicate whether Defendants obtained a building permit for the building. Defendants expanded their business to allow the rental of sites for camping trailers and tents. Gradually more sites were added, eventually growing to about 20 picnic-camping sites.

Defendants then started to erect additional sanitary facilities, consisting of toilets and showers, on the land and more grading and landscaping to further increase the capacity for more camping sites, and larger sites for bigger recreational vehicles. Defendants were informed by the County Planning Department that, because a business use was involved, the building permit could not be issued until a Conditional Use Permit was applied for and obtained from the County Commission. Defendants sought the Conditional Use Permit, and were eventually granted a variance, recognizing that the campground use was a legal nonconforming use which Defendants had a right to continue, but concluding that Defendants had no right to enlarge its camping operation.

Defendants challenged that determination. The County also brought an abatement proceeding. In the consolidated cases, the trial court upheld the County's determination.

It is well-recognized law that, if before the adoption of the zoning ordinance, the defendants had established a use as a picnic and camping park, they acquired a vested right to continue that use thereafter as a nonconforming use.

A legal nonconforming use has been defined as authority granted to the owner to use his property in a manner otherwise violative of the zoning regulations. In other words, it is in the nature of a waiver of the strict letter of the zoning ordinance without sacrifice to its spirit and purpose. Over the ensuing years Defendants have properly relied on the nonconforming use, thus acquiring a vested right which could not be affected or changed after the nonconforming use was granted.

Having thus acquired a nonconforming use to use their 14-acre tract as a picnic and camping park, any regulation of the county zoning ordinance which would prevent that use did not apply to Defendants' 14-acre tract.

Hence the issue presented on this appeal, which is whether Defendants can rent space for recreational vehicles and other camping trailers, cannot be resolved by a determination of whether such trailers come within the zoning ordinance that regulates the use of "trailers and/or mobile homes" in this district of the County. Rather, the issue is whether the use of such trailers is a method ordinarily and reasonably adopted to make the original use granted to Defendants available to them without constituting a substantial change in the nature and purpose of that original use, or whether, on the contrary, the use of these trailers would constitute such a departure from the original use as to constitute a new and impermissible use.

The burden of establishing that the use in question is fundamentally the same use and not a new and impermissible one is on the party asserting it. This is in accordance with the general policy of zoning to carefully limit the extension and enlargement of nonconforming uses. However, the use cannot be interpreted in such a way as to unlawfully reduce the original vested interest acquired by the nonconforming use.

We feel that some amount of latitude must be allowed a nonconforming use for reasonable expansion and the maintenance of accessory uses. Businesses should not be prevented from staying competitive in their respective markets by expanding or evolving in the modern world. The fact that improved and more efficient or different instrumentalities are used in the operation of the use does not preclude the use made from being a continuation of the prior nonconforming use, provided that such means are ordinarily and reasonably adapted to make the established use available to the owners and so long as the original nature and purpose of the undertaking remain unchanged.

The determination of whether the use challenged is substantially the same kind of use as that which was originally obtained is necessarily based in large measure on the facts and circumstances of the particular case. In deciding whether the particular activity is within the scope of the established or acquired nonconforming use, consideration may be given to, among others, the following factors:

(1) To what extent does the use in question reflect the nature and purpose of the prevailing nonconforming use?

(2) Is it merely a different manner of utilizing the same use or does it constitute a use different in character, nature, and kind?

(3) Does this use have a substantially different effect on the neighborhood?

The degree to which the original nature and purpose of the undertaking remains unchanged largely determines whether there has been a change in the preexisting use.

We are unable to say on the record before us that the decision of the trial court was based on a finding and ruling that the renting of spaces by Defendants on their 14-acre tract for more and larger recreational vehicles would constitute such a change in, or enlargement of, the use of their land for the granted use of a picnic and camping park as to amount to the substitution of a new and different use. The case is remanded for disposition in accordance with the principles enunciated in this opinion.

Reversed and remanded.

PT-A: SELECTED ANSWER 1

MEMORANDUM

TO: Lou Estepe

FROM: Applicant

SUBJECT: Tehama County v. Tepee Campground

DATE: July 29, 2014

Introduction

This memorandum is an objective analysis as to the legal issues raised by the Notice to Abate filed by Tehama County Attorney Al Read against our client, Jane Maya. The analysis below will discuss the charges raised in the Notice to Abate. Additionally, the analysis below will examine the controlling law and apply the facts of this matter to such law. Moreover, in anticipation of opposing counsel's arguments, the weight of the best opposing views shall be made in order to fully assess the strength and likelihood of success of arguments that are advantageous to our client and arguments that are adverse.

Analysis

I.   WHETHER RECREATIONAL PARK TRAILERS WILL BE CLASSIFIED ALONG THE LINES OF A RECREATIONAL VEHICLE OR A STRUCTURE, SUBJECT TO THE BUILDING CODE.

The first charge in the Notice to Abate is that the Recreational Park Trailers (RPTs) owned by Maya are permanent structures, in violation of the Land Development Regulation (LDR) § 222.1. According to LDR § 222.1, campgrounds are defined as "establishments providing overnight or short-term sites for recreational vehicles, campers or tents, that have no permanent structures other than a management office, laundry, small grocery, storage facility, and sanitary facilities that shall be solely for the occupants of the campground." At issue, as stated by the record, is whether an RPT can be considered a permanent structure.

There appear to be two methods of analysis in terms of determining the characterization of an RPT: (1) that the RPT should be governed by the same standards as the RV; or (2) that the RPT is a permanent structure or manufactured home and should be treated as such. Clearly Maya will advocate for the first argument, while the County will advocate for the second argument.

A.   RPTs Appear to Have Similar Use and Structure to Recreational Vehicles, Which Are Not Classified as Permanent Structures.

The Federal Manufacturered Home Construction & Safety Standards Act does not classify RVs as regulated by the federal government as structures or manufactured homes. 24 C.F.R. § 3282.8(g). The definition that the federal statute uses in defining RVs is: (1) built on a single chassis; (2) 400 square feet or less when measured at the largest horizontal projection; (3) self-propelled or permanently towable by a light duty truck; (4) designed primarily not for use as a permanent dwelling, but as a temporary living quarters for recreational, camping, travel, or seasonal use. Id.

In Tall Timbers Resort v. Oregon Construction Department (2010), the court dealt with a very similar matter and ultimately ended up holding that the Oregon Construction Department's determination as to the classification of an RPT deserved deference. There, the Department adopted new regulations which determined that RPTs were subject to the state's construction code. In suit brought by a seller of RPTs, the owner of a campground in which RPTs were installed, and the owners of an RPT, the parties sought to have that decision overturned by the court. As part of its reasoning, the court noted that the Construction Code provisions must receive liberal construction to advance its purposes, generally centered in matters affecting health, safety, and welfare.

The parties bringing challenge notes that RPTs meet many of the same standards as promulgated by the federal RV standards in 24 C.F.R. § 3282.8(g). Moreover, they noted that the principal difference between the RPT and RVC is that the RPT covers all requirements found in the building code but the RV does not. However, the court noted that there is a significant difference between an RV and an RPT; namely, that an RPT is "intended for installation in a 'park.'" Tall Timbers at 8. Moreover, the court, after hearing arguments regarding whether or not an RPT should or should not be classified as a structure, ultimately deferred to the finding of the Department. The court stated that "the Department has determined that RPTs are structures, even if primarily designed to provide temporary living quarters for recreational, camping, or seasonal use." Id. at 8-9. Accordingly, since the court deemed the finding reasonable, the court upheld that decision.

Here, the first argument that Maya will want to make is establishing the status quo as it pertains to the regulation of RPTs within Tehama County. First, she will want to argue that the Planning Department and County Commission never decided whether or not an RPT is a structure. Thus, while the court in Tall Timbers was deferential to the finding of the Department, no such deference should be afforded here because there is no finding upon which to rely. Second, she will want to argue that the Tehama County Building Code has no provisions on RPTs or RVs at all. In fact, the Tehama County Building Department has never issued a building permit or inspected an RPT before or after installation. Moreover, the building code does not make any distinctions between the types of RVs, irrespective whether they are fifth wheels, towable trailers, or motor homes: it considers them all RVs. In addition, in a memo from the Director of the Building Department within Tehama County, the Director states that RPTs pose less of a risk to the public than RVs. Further, the Director goes on to advocate that RPTs should not be subject to any regulations that the County is not willing to subject RVs to. As a result, based on the status quo, Maya has a reasonable argument that, in light of the absence of any provisions in Tehama County that are applicable to this situation, the federal regulations regarding RVs should control.

To that end, under 24 C.F.R. § 3282.8(g), Maya can argue that the RPTs at issue also meet the guidelines promulgated by the statute. First, the facts indicate that Maya's RPTs are built on a single chassis. Second, based on the measurements provided, Maya's RPTs are 395 square feet. Third, the RPTs have wheels and can be towed by light-duty pickup trucks. This fact is supported by the Recreational Park Trailer Industry Association's letter, in which their Executive Director makes clear that RPTs are able to be transported on roads and highways. Finally, as indicated by the facts, Maya intends to have the RPT leased for short-term camping use, as opposed to long term or permanent residence. Using Tall Timbers as an example, Maya will also have to overcome the distinction between an objective or subjective use of the dwelling. Under either standard, Maya will have a compelling argument. Under the objective standard, Maya can argue that the RPT only lends itself to short-term leases because it is not designed nor created to be a permanent dwelling. Indeed, the RPTs are nice and come with nicer amenities than a typical RV. However, the fact remains that these are not intended or designed to be used for permanent residences, particularly with installation at a campground. Moreover, while she does intend to rent them out year long, she will have to argue that this is a showing of successive short-term residences, rather than one long-term, permanent residence. This is supported by the fact that the unit would consistently be turned over for the next guest after the prior guest vacates. Additionally, under the subjective analysis, Maya can argue that, as the individual leasing the RPTs out, she does not have the subjective intent to make the RPTs a permanent residence for anyone.

As a result, since Maya is able to satisfy both the requirements in Tehama County and show that her RPTs meet federal standards for RVs, she has a reasonable argument that Tehama County should recognize her RPTs as RVs.

B.   RPTs Have Many Similar Qualities to Manufactured Homes and Could be Considered Structures.

On the other hand, the County has a reasonable argument that they should treat RPTs as structures. While the County will have to concede that its building code does not cover RPTs or RVs, the thrust of their argument will rely on the fact that the RPT shares many common characteristics with a permanent structure and should be regulated as such.

The County will have to rely on Tall Timbers, mainly because its holding is advantageous. There, in arguing that an RPT should be treated as a structure, the Oregon Department of Construction argued that an RPT had the following characteristics: (1) has a combination of the same types of materials used in any home and involves all the same safety issues as a home; (2) intended for the same type of occupancy as any other vacation home; (3) structure with enclosed external walls; (4) clearly designed for housing or shelter and it is arranged for the support of individuals; and (5) it is equipped with plumbing, electrical, and mechanical systems just as is any dwelling. Id. at 7. Moreover, the court noted the findings of the Department in that RPTs were "generally constructed in the same manner as single family dwellings," "arrives already assembled," and usually found in the location in which they are parked for an extended duration of time. Id. at 6.

Here, the County will point to what is known of Maya's RPTs. First, Maya's RPTs present a lot of the same features as a home would have: a fully functioning kitchen, bathroom, bedrooms, and even a fireplace. The County will highlight the fact that such a structure should be subject to building codes for the safety of those inside, particularly if a fireplace is involved. Second, the County will argue that an RPT is intended for the same type of dwelling as a vacation home, regardless of the term of lease. They will attempt to distinguish this from an RV, which necessitates that the individual drive the vehicle to the desired location. Here, like any other rental home, the structure is already present and the individuals who seek to use the RPT must come to the RPT itself. The County will argue this is operatively no different than having a vacation home. Moreover, the County will have to point to the findings of the Staff Report for the CUP in that the RPT presents a similar situation as a motel, mainly because they arrive in a passenger vehicle, stay a limited time, leave, and the RPT is then cleaned out and turned over for the next guest. Third, the County will argue that the paneling on the outside of the RPT has the tendency of showing that it is more like a home than a vehicle. This argument may not be that compelling, as RVs certainly have paneling as well. Fourth, as already shown, the existence of amenities gives off the impression that it is for shelter. In fact, Maya indicates that she intends the RPTs to create an environment in which guests are "camping" but really still have "comforts" such as running water, high definition TV, and feathered pillows. The County will argue that those are indicative of a shelter, rather than an RV. Finally, it is undisputed that an RPT hooks into sewer systems and draws power from the electrical grid. Unlike RVs which carry their own generator and have their own power support, the County will argue that an RPT is no different than a home which essentially plops down and begins utilizing resources for the purposes of permanent establishment.

Ultimately, in the absence of additional legal authority, this issue could really go either way. The court in Tall Timbers was really deferential as to the finding of the Department. In the absence of such a finding here, the court is going to need to make a determination on its own. The major advantage that Maya has for her argument is the amount of support she has from various groups: including the Director of the Building Department and the Recreational Trailer Park Industry Association. Moreover, since the status quo appears to have a gap in the statutory framework regarding the regulation of RVs and RPTs, the fact that federal legislation is present can be instructive for the court. As a result, it is likely that the court sides with Maya in viewing the RPTs as having similar use to RVs, thereby avoiding regulation as structures under the building code.

II.   WHETHER MAYA'S USE OF RPTS CONSTITUTES AN ENLARGEMENT OF A NONCONFORMING USE, AN IMPERMISSIBLE MATERIAL INCREASE OF INTENSITY IN THE NONCONFORMING USE, OR A CHANGE TO ANOTHER NONCONFORMING USE THAT IS NOT MATERIALLY LESS IN INTENSITY.

It is well-recognized law that, if before the adoption of a zoning ordinance, a party had established a use as a camping park, they acquired a vested right to continue that use thereafter as a nonconforming use. County of Los Banos v. Leskiewicz (2000). Generally a legal nonconforming use has been defined as authority granted to the owner to use his property in a manner otherwise violative of the zoning regulations. Id.

Here, in 1994, the current Tehama LDRs were adopted and all properties within the County were rezoned. As part of this rezoning process, the Tepee Campground was zoned into an area that was zoned rural/residential. Within such zoning districts, any campgrounds that wanted to be created after the zoning districts were created requires a Conditional Use Permit (CUP). However, since Tepee Campground had been in existence since the mid-1970s, they were permitted to be a nonconforming use under LDR § 540. In 1979, Tepee Campground had a total of 142 campsites, with 33 tent sites and 109 RV sites on 7.9 acres, with other minor structures totaling 5,100 square feet. To date, the facts indicate that Tepee Campground is essentially unchanged with regards to its size or the number of its respective camp or RV sites.

The Notice of Abate has three potential violations of the Tepee Campground nonconforming use: (1) that the RPTs are an enlargement of the nonconforming use; (2) the use of RPTs is a nonconforming use that has materially increased in intensity; or (3) that the nonconforming use has been substituted for another nonconforming use and such new nonconforming use is not materially less intense than the prior nonconforming use. Each shall be analyzed separately.

A.   The Use of RPTs at Tepee Campground Cannot and Will Not Be Viewed as an Enlargement of the Nonconforming Use.

This argument is by far the weakest on behalf of the County. As stated above, from 1979 to the present date, Tepee Campground has essentially remained unchanged. They have not acquired any new land and have not expanded beyond the original 7.9 acres that they originally inhabited in 1979. In fact, in the Staff Report, the County essentially concedes that aerial photography indicates the current configuration of the campground is almost identical to the 1978 layout. Moreover, the facts are clear as it pertains to the use of RPTs. Maya is only using the RPTs on 54 of the 109 sites that she has. She is not adding 54 more spots to her 109. Moreover, her use of less than half of the slots she already has available cannot possibly be considered an expansion of her already existing nonconforming use. Additionally, the fact that the slots are used for the very same purpose of short-term camping, while also maintaining some sort of recreational vehicle on the land, does not expand the use of her property because the activity is occurring on lots that were already present. In addition, the RPTs are no bigger than many, if not most RVs. As a result, the actual footprint or the structure floor area of the pads need not expand and in some cases, may actually shrink in size. Finally, there is nothing in the factual record that indicates that Maya intends to expand her existing pads.

As a result, it is likely beyond dispute that the use of her already existing RV lots for the purposes of RPTs does not constitute an enlargement of her nonconforming use.

B.   The Use of RPTs Will Likely Not Constitute a Material Increase in Intensity.

Generally, this is a fact intensive inquiry guided by LDR § 541.4 which states that intensity shall "include a consideration of traffic generated, perceived level of activity, operational characteristics, and potentially adverse impacts on neighboring lands."

1. Traffic Generated

Here, Maya may offer the traffic impact assessment that was provided with her application. In this assessment, it is stated that the proposed use of RPTs on Tepee Campground will slightly reduce vehicle traffic flow on the West Bank Road, introduce no increase in traffic impacts, and provide more than adequate vehicular site access. Moreover, the assessment indicates that the number of recreational vehicles accessing and exiting the property would likely decrease. There does not appear to be any evidence contained in the factual record with which the County will be able to rebut this perceived benefit. As a result, Maya should be able to show that there will be no traffic increase as a result of the use of RPTs.

2. Perceived Level of Activity

Here, the County could present the remainder of the traffic impact assessment which asserts that there will be an increase in the number of overall patrons at Tepee Campground. Moreover, based on the increase of foot traffic, there is a concern raised by the Staff Report for the CUP that was later withdrawn, that Maya would be able to, at some point down the road, convert part or all of the campground into a mobile home park. This could drastically increase the perceived level of activity and be a direct violation of the zoning ordinance. Ultimately, since the concerns here are only speculative, and there does not appear to be any evidence in the record that affirmatively establishes that the perceived level of activity is something that is adverse to the interests of the zoning ordinance, this should not be a bar to Maya using RPTs on her property.

3. Operational Characteristics

Here, as mentioned above, Maya can show that her overall footprint with the use of RPTs will be less than that of using RVs. She is already using 54 of her lots and RPTs take up considerably less space than that of her RVs. However, the County can argue that since an RPT must be plugged into the power grid and use the sewage system, that its operation is more of a burden than an RV, which would be a stand alone entity. Moreover, the County will argue that she is changing the operational characteristics of her land by essentially changing what was a campground into a resort. The facts indicate that she was charging $27.50 a night for guests to park their RV. Now, in order to park their RPT, she will be charging anywhere from $175 to $300 per night to rent an RPT. The County will argue that this is a change in operational characteristics such that it should be impermissible. However, it is difficult to see how the cost per patron will increase the intensity of the nonconforming use. Ultimately, in light of the argument below, it is likely that Maya will also prevail on this argument since she is not really changing her operational structure to accommodate for the RPTs.

4. Adverse Impacts on Neighboring Lands

Here, Maya will be able to point to the Air Quality and Fuel Consumption Analysis for RPTs prepared by Science for Hire. The report indicates that replacing one traditional RV site with one RPT site could save approximately 9,500 gallons of fuel and reduce the CO2 emissions in the atmosphere by 363,000 pounds a year. Scaled to accommodate for the replacement of 54 sites with RPTs, it would save 513,000 gallons of fuel and reduce carbon emissions by 9,801 tons annually. There is no doubt that the reduction of carbon emissions into the atmosphere is a beneficial aspect to neighboring lands, as opposed to an adverse impact. Moreover, Maya will argue that since there is public transportation nearby, it is likely that these figures could increase as people will take public transit to Tepee Campground.

As a result, since the facts tend to indicate that the use of RPTs is not a nonconforming use that materially increases in intensity, Maya should be able to carry the burden of satisfying LDR § 541.2.

C.   Whether the Change to RPTs Will Be Considered a Change to a Different Nonconforming Use.

The final charge by the County is that Maya's use of RPTs is a change from an authorized nonconforming use to another nonconforming use in violation of LDR § 541.3. A plain reading of the statute indicates two showings that must be made: (1) whether a change occurred; and (2) whether that change is materially less intense than the prior nonconforming use.

Generally, "the burden of establishing that the use in question is fundamentally the same use and not a new and impermissible one is on the party asserting it." Los Banos at 13. As a result, Maya will have the burden of establishing that the use of RPTs on Tepee Campground is the same nonconforming use or, at the very least, a change that is permissible because it is materially less intense.

1.   Has a Change Occurred?

In Los Banos, the court grappled with whether a present nonconforming use had been substantially changed to another nonconforming use. There, after a zoning ordinance, the defendants had improved a 14 acre land by trimming trees, removing and burning brush, grading, erecting retaining walls, building a road, installing a cesspool, and erecting an outhouse. After their business expanded, they let individuals rent land for bringing camping trailers and tents. The County brought action asserting that such use expanded their nonconforming use and alternatively, that it was a material change in the property. The appellate court ultimately remanded for further investigation and development of the facts. However, in so doing, the court listed three factors as a guide to determining whether the nonconforming use had been substantially changed: (1) to what extent does the use in question reflect the nature and purpose of the prevailing nonconforming use; (2) is it merely a different manner of utilizing the same use or does it constitute a use different in character, nature and kind; and (3) does the use have a substantially different effect on the neighborhood. Id. at 13. Moreover, the court articulated that "the degree to which the original nature and purpose of the undertaking remains unchanged largely determines whether there has been a change in the preexisting use." Id. at 14.

Here, Maya will argue that the use of RPTs does not change the nature of the nonconforming use of Tepee Campground. First, she will argue that the use of RPTs is a direct reflection of the nonconforming use, which is ultimately a campground. She will point to the original plot of land that was used as Tepee Campground to show that the same 109 RV slots are the slots that are currently used to house the 54 RPTs. The essential characteristic of the land has not changed: she is allowing people to camp on her campground in recreational vehicles. Second, Maya will argue that it is the same use because there is operatively no difference between RVs and RPTs. As discussed in great length above, RPTs and RVs share many characteristics in terms of the way they are constructed. Moreover, the way they are utilized, as a recreational vehicle from which to camp from, is essentially the same. Finally, as articulated above, the use of RPTs does have a substantial effect on the neighborhood: one of providing a benefit. In fact, the facts clearly indicate that neighbors and nearby businesses "have supported the appearance of the attractive wood sided RPTs and the enhanced landscaping." Thus, in addition to the fact that the RPTs are, on the whole, better for the environment, they are also better to look at.

On the other hand, the County will argue everything to the contrary. First, the County will argue that the use of RPTs changes everything about the use of the campground. The County will point to the fact that Maya intends to create a resort named "Solitude," as opposed to maintaining a campground. Moreover, her vision is the creation of "Glamping," which is a form of glamorous camping, a cross between staying in a hotel and camping. This is a change of significance from the prevailing nonconforming use, which would be primarily a campground. Second, there is a wholly new use for the property. The County will argue that when Maya was just using the spaces for RVs, she was charging $27.50 per night for visitors to park their RV at her campsite. Now, with the use of RPTs, she will be charging customers somewhere between $175 and $300 per night. The County will argue that this is more of a change to a resort than it is to maintaining a campsite. Finally, the County will rely on the fact that since RVs came with their own generators, the fact that RPTs have to be plugged into the grid and use the sewage system adversely affects the neighborhood.

As a result, the court will likely side with Maya in this argument. Although it is possible to see that the introduction of RPTs could constitute a material change to the former nonconforming use, the fact that Maya has not really altered any aspect of the land and that she is still using the campground as a campground should bolster her argument over the objections raised by the County. However, the disparity in cost between an RV and RPT rental is quite large and could prove to be dispositive.

2.   Is the Change Materially Less Intense Than the Prior Nonconforming Use?

For many of the same reasons articulated above, this issue will turn on a determination as to which of the factors the court weighs in more heavily. Maya's best arguments are that the traffic in the area will decrease as a result of the use of RPTs and the carbon footprint and gas emissions will reduce substantially. The County will argue that this opens the door for Maya to essentially create a permanent trailer park and that the operational characteristics of using the RPTs will be a bigger toll on the public resources in the area. However the court comes out above will likely be how the court comes out on this issue as well.

As a result, since Maya is using the campground for much of the same purpose as she was prior to the introduction of RPTs, it is unlikely that the court will find her use of the land with RPTs to be a change in nonconforming use. Even if the court does find that it is a new nonconforming use, based on the arguments presented, it is likely that the court will find that the new nonconforming use of using RPTs is materially less intense than the use of RVs. As a result, Maya's nonconforming use should be permissible.

III.   CONCLUSION

Therefore, Maya has a pretty good argument that the RPT should be viewed as an RV in line with the federal statutes, in light of the absence of any regulations within Tehama County. Moreover, with the level of support she appears to get from various administrative agencies within Tehama County, she should be able to show that the court should side with the federal statutes, rather than give deference to an administrative body that has made no determination as to the classification of RPTs. While Tehama County does have an equally reasonable argument, based on the fact that RPTs share many characteristics with permanent structures, the absence of any local rules might prove fatal for their argument.

Additionally, Maya should be successful in rebutting the charge that her use of RPTs expands her nonconforming use because the facts unequivocally show that the campground has remained unchanged since 1978. Additionally, Maya has a reasonable argument on the merits that her use of the land with RPTs is not a material increase in intensity of the nonconforming use because RPTs take up less space, will result in less traffic, and are better for the environment. Finally, Maya should be able to show that her use of the RPTs does not substantially change her nonconforming use. However, if the court finds that it does, based on the same material increase in intensity analysis, Maya should be able to show that such use is permissible.

PT-A: SELECTED ANSWER 2

To: Lou Estepe

From: Applicant

Subject: Tehama County v. Tepee Campground

Date: July 29, 2014

MEMORANDUM

You asked me to write an objective memorandum discussing and analyzing the charges made in the Notice of Abatement. You also asked me to evaluate our chances of prevailing against each charge. I have provided such below.

There are two charges made in the Notice of Abatement: 1. That the Recreational Park Trailers (RPTs) are permanent structures in violation of the Land Development Regulations (LDR); and 2. That the RPTs are an enlargement, expansion, or material increase in intensity of a nonconforming use; or a change to another nonconforming use that is not a materially less intense use. I have addressed each charge separately below.

Charge One: The RPTs Are Permanent Structure in Violation of LDR

Section 222.1 states that "campground use means establishments providing overnight or short-term sites for recreational vehicles, trailers, campers or tents, that have no permanent structures other than a management office, laundry, small grocery, storage facility, and sanitary facilities that shall be solely for the occupants of the campground."

The County is likely to argue that RPTs are permanent structures that violate LDR Section 222.1 as the RPTs will not serve as a management office, laundry, small grocery, storage facility, or sanitary facility. The County is likely to cite to many of the arguments made in Tall Timbers Resort v. Oregon Construction Department that RPTs were structures. The County is likely to argue that the fact that RPTs use the same type of materials as homes, serves the same function as any other vacation home, has exterior walls, and can act as a permanent home for individuals makes them structures.

The County is likely to rely heavily on the fact that the court in Tall Timbers ruled in favor of the Oregon Construction Department, who was arguing in favor of classifying an RPT as a structure. However, that case is distinguishable from the instant case in many ways. The first is the basis for the Court's decision. In ruling in favor for the Oregon Construction Department, the Court did not consider in great detail any of the factors presented by either side with respect to whether an RPT could be classified as a structure or manufactured home and therefore subject to the Construction Code. The Court was very clear in stating that its decision was based in substantial part on the fact that the Oregon Supreme Court had previously ruled that the Construction Code Act's provisions "must receive liberal construction to advance its purpose." Tall Timbers. In that case, the Construction Department itself had already determined that RPTs were subject to the State Uniform Construction Code. Since the Code was required to receive liberal construction, the court stated that its only job was to determine whether the determination that RPTs fall within the Construction Code's definition of "structure" was "plainly unreasonable" or not. The Court determined that it was not.

Further, this case is from Oregon, not Columbia. It therefore is only persuasive in nature and not binding authority. The County will find it difficult to demonstrate many similarities between Tall Timbers and the instant case. Unlike in Tall Timbers, the director of the Building Department in Tehama County does not make any distinction between RPTs and RVs, and therefore does not consider the Building Code to regulate RPTs. Additionally, the HUD Office on Manufacturered Housing also does not regulate RPTs in any fashion. Since there is no regulation of RPTs under either code, it will be difficult for the County to use the outcome in Tall Timbers to support their argument as there is no code here that must be given "liberal construction." The Columbia Supreme Court has not even made such a requirement, either. Since there is no clear definition of RPTs in Columbia, the court's decision will necessarily be determined on the facts.

As stated previously, the County is likely to argue that an RPT is a structure because it uses the same material as a house, it is connected to the ground, and it serves the same function as another vacation home.

Maya can counter by arguing that an RPT is more similar to an RV as the RPT construction standards set by the RPT industry fits all the criteria of RVs set forth by federal regulation 24 C.F.R Section 3282.8(g), namely an RPT must be "limited to 400 square feet, built on a single chassis, mounted on wheels, and must comply with various requirements for electrical, plumbing, and heating systems." Conditional Use Permit Application Staff Report. Additionally, Maya can use the arguments set forth by the Recreational Park Trailer Industry Association to support her argument that an RPT should be considered an RV and not a structure. In particular, Maya should point to the fact that a judicial finding that RPTs are "structures" could have mass impact on the campground industry across the nation. She can argue that such a decision would make it possible for other courts to approve restrictions on RVs as well, as there is no discernable distinction between RPTs and RVs.

Maya can also argue that there is already precedence to consider RPTs RVs in other states. She can note that, so long as an RPT meets industry standards, it is treated as a vehicle in other states. She can argue that this tendency for states to classify RPTs as RVs is a growing trend across the nation, and since the court in the instant case does not have any binding prior authority to draw from in Columbia state law, it should consider national trends.

The County here makes a strong argument for why RPTs should be considered a structure. However, Maya seems to have an almost equally strong argument for why they should be considered vehicles instead. Given that Maya has the additional arguments that a finding of an RPT as a structure could have a massive impact on the camping industry across the nation and that the national trend seems to be to recognize conforming RPTs as vehicles, it is likely that the court will hold that an RPT is not a permanent structure within the meaning of the LDR and therefore does not violate Section 222.1

Charge Two: The RPTs Are An Enlargement, Expansion, or Material Increase in Intensity of a Nonconforming Use; or a Change to Another Nonconforming Use That is Not a Materially Less Intense Use

LDR Section 540 states that nonconforming use is any use of land which was established pursuant to the zoning and building laws in effect at the time of its development, but which use is not permitted by the current LDRs for the zoning district in which it is located. It states that those nonconforming uses that were permitted by right at the time of its development are permitted nonconforming uses. Section 540 goes on to state that a conditional use permit will not be required to continue the existing nonconforming use, however, a conditional use permit will be required for any change of use. LDR Section 541 lists the different ways, use, or characteristics of the activity can be changed. These ways are: 1. Enlarging or expanding in areas of structure or land occupied; 2. Materially increasing the intensity of the use; or 3. Changing the nonconforming use to another nonconforming use unless any new use is a materially less intense nonconforming use. The County is likely to argue each of these changes. I have addressed each individually below.

Has the Use of Recreational Park Trailers (RPTs) Enlarged or Expanded Maya's Nonconforming Use of Her Land?

The County is likely to argue that the use of RPTs will enlarge or expand the use of Tepee Campground as a camping location, and Maya therefore must obtain a CUP. The County will likely cite multiple complaints from neighbors that the campground has increased its number of sites over the years. The County may also try to argue enlargement or expansion because, unlike Recreational Vehicles (RVs), RPTs are permanent fixtures and connected to the ground. There will therefore be no point in time where these lots are empty.

Maya may counter by arguing that the county is unable to substantiate the neighbors' complaint about expansion, as aerial photography shows that the current layout is virtually identical to the layout when the camp opened in 1978. She will also argue that she is not adding any new campsites. Rather, she is replacing 54 RV sites with RPTs. She can also point out that RPTs take up significantly less space than RVs. RVs can be up to 78 feet long, whereas RPTs are only 39 feet long, 12 feet wide, and about 395 square feet. Therefore she is decreasing the size of the vehicles that are located in existing spots.

The County's point that the RPTs would be permanently located in the spots rather than RVs is a valid argument. This could prevail. However, given the fact that Maya is not adding any new sites, and that it is feasible (and likely, according to Maya) that RVs could occupy those spaces full time as well, it is more likely that the County's argument will fail. Therefore, the court is unlikely to consider the use of RPTs as enlarging or expanding Maya's nonconforming use of her land to the extent that she is required to obtain a CUP.

Has the Use of RPTs Materially Increased the Intensity of the Use?

Section 541.4 states that "the determination of the level of intensity shall include consideration of traffic generated, perceived level of activity, operational characteristics and potentially adverse impacts on neighboring lands."

The traffic impact assessment of the RPT change is likely to help our case. It states that the change to RPTs is likely to slightly reduce vehicle traffic flow into the campground as a result of a reduction in the number of RVs on the road and increase of passenger cars. The county may try to argue that it will negatively impact traffic because the change will likely increase the number of patrons using the campground. However, Maya can counter by pointing out that the use of RPTs will reduce the number of RVs that are in the area. Instead of RVs there will be passenger cars, which are easier to drive on the roads, making them safer. While there may be an increase in perceived level of activity, it's unlikely that the increase in patrons using the land is sufficient to warrant a material increase that would require the need for a conditional use permit.

Nor is the change likely to have potentially adverse impacts on neighboring lands. The County can try to argue that there will be a negative impact because now the campgrounds will essentially be a mobile home park now, however Maya can counter by arguing that the lot is currently routinely filled by RVs which are substantially less aesthetically appealing than the RPTs. She can also argue that the switch to RPTs will have a positive impact on the local environment, since it is likely to save approximately 513,000 gallons of fuel a year and reduce the CO_2 emissions released into the atmosphere by 19,602,000 pounds each year as a result of the decrease of RV use. Maya can also argue that, unlike RVs, RPTs do not make any noise, meaning that the neighbors will not have to deal with as much noise from the campground anymore.

Given that the change to RPTs is likely to decrease RV traffic, improve environmental conditions, and eradicate both visual and noise nuisance, it is unlikely that the county will be able to prove that the change to RPTs has materially increased the intensity of the use of the campground to the extent that Maya should be required to obtain a CUP.

Has the Use of RPTS Changed the Nonconforming Use to Another Nonconforming Use?

Generally, if any change converts a nonconforming use to another nonconforming use, the owner will need to obtain a conditional use permit before such use may be permitted. However if the use is fundamentally the same, a conditional use permit will not be necessary in order for the use to be permitted. The burden of establishing that the use in question is "fundamentally the same" use and not another nonconforming use is "on the party asserting it." We, therefore, bear the burden of showing that Maya's use of RPTS does not change the nonconforming use of Tepee Campground.

Tepee campground was created in the mid-1970s. It has continuously been used as a campground ever since. When the Tehama County adopted the current LDRs in 1994, Tepee Campground was located in a district zoned rural/residential. Since Tepee campground was already in existence, its use as a campground is considered a permitted nonconforming use that does not require a conditional use permit (CUP). So long as Tepee campground continues to be used for the same nonconforming use, it will not need to obtain a CUP. County of Los Banos v. Leskiewicz.

A new use of land will not be considered a change to another nonconforming use if the new use does not make a "substantial change in the nature and purpose of" the original use. Leskiewicz. To determine whether the new use is within the scope of the established nonconforming use, the following factors are considered: 1. the extent that the new use reflects the "nature and purpose of the prevailing nonconforming use"; 2. whether it is merely a different manner of making the same use or whether the new use is "different in character, nature, and kind"; and 3. whether the new use has a "substantially different effect" on the surrounding area. Leskiewicz. The greatest amount of weight is afforded to the first factor. Leskiewicz.

Maya can argue that using RPTs does not in any way change the nonconforming use of the campground. She can argue that the nonconforming use was to allow customers to come to the campground, stay for a few nights to camp, enjoying nature, and then leave. The RPTs do not change this purpose at all. It functions the same as if the customers were staying in tents. All it changes is how nice the tents are. The County is likely to argue that the use of RPTs completely changes the use of land, transforming it from a campground into a hotel or even a mobile home park, citing Maya's intentions to create a resort called "Solitude." The County will argue that a resort is not the same thing as camping; therefore it is a whole different nonconforming use.

However, this argument is likely to fail. It has been previously held that, in order for a new use to qualify under an already existing nonuse, it need not be exactly the same. Rather, some "latitude" must be afforded for "reasonable expansion." Leskiewicz.

Specifically, Leskiewicz held that a "business should not be prevented from staying competitive" by "expanding or evolving in the modern world." Maya can argue that this is exactly what she is doing. She will point out that she is unlikely to be able to stay open for many more years if she must continue to allow purely RVs as soaring gas prices will likely decrease RV use in the near future. They are therefore necessary in order for her to stay competitive in her industry, as many campsites across the country are starting to use RPTs. Her resort is a move into "glamping," the future that the camping industry is naturally moving towards. The County may try to argue that including modern creature comforts, such as indoor plumbing and a flat screen TV, defeat the purpose of camping, however the court is likely to disregard this argument as RVs already often make use of both technologies.

Maya will also emphasize that the RPTs are still meant for temporary visits, and that they allow customers to appreciate nature more than RVs ever could. Therefore RPTs are just a different way of making the most enjoying nature and camping, and is not different in character, nature, or kind. Maya will also argue that the new use does not have a substantially different effect on the surrounding area. Given these arguments, as well as the discussion concerning the effect this change will have on the surrounding community made in previous sections, Maya is likely to meet her burden here in showing that the new use of RPTs does not fundamentally change the use of Tepee Campgrounds into a use other than camping. It is very likely that the judge will not consider the use of RPTs a change to another nonconforming use here.

Conclusion

While the County does have a number of strong arguments to support their two charges, for the reasons and arguments stated above, it is likely that we will prevail against both charges. Please let me know if you would like me to conduct any further research on this matter.

July 2014

California
Bar
Examination

Performance Test B
INSTRUCTIONS AND FILE

RILEY INSTRUMENTS V. LRI, INC.

RILEY INSTRUMENTS, INC. v. LRI, INC.

INSTRUCTIONS

1. This performance test is designed to evaluate your ability to handle a select number of legal authorities in the context of a factual problem involving a client.

2. The problem is set in the fictional State of Columbia, one of the United States.

3. You will have two sets of materials with which to work: a File and a Library.

4. The File contains factual materials about your case. The first document is a memorandum containing the instructions for the tasks you are to complete.

5. The Library contains the legal authorities needed to complete the tasks. The case reports may be real, modified, or written solely for the purpose of this performance test. If the cases appear familiar to you, do not assume that they are precisely the same as you have read before. Read each thoroughly, as if it were new to you. You should assume that cases were decided in the jurisdictions and on the dates shown. In citing cases from the Library, you may use abbreviations and omit page citations.

6. You should concentrate on the materials provided, but you should also bring to bear on the problem your general knowledge of the law. What you have learned in law school and elsewhere provides the general background for analyzing the problem; the File and Library provide the specific materials with which you must work.

7. Although there are no restrictions on how you apportion your time, you should probably allocate at least 90 minutes to reading and organizing before you begin preparing your response.

8. Your response will be graded on its compliance with instructions and on its content, thoroughness, and organization.

MARTIN, RIVERA & TRAN, LLP

Attorneys and Counselors at Law

Eagle Point, Columbia

INTEROFFICE MEMORANDUM

TO: Applicant

FROM: Helen Rivera

RE: Riley Instruments, Inc. v. LRI, Inc.

DATE: July 31, 2014

On May 12, 2014, we received the Final Decision and Award of Arbitrator Stanley Warren ruling in favor of our client, Riley Instruments, Inc. Later we realized that Arbitrator Warren had failed to address one of the issues that we had submitted to him and that he had also failed to award us attorney's fees. We brought these matters to his attention on May 27, 2014. Over the objection of Mark Stilton, the attorney for the defendant LRI, Inc., Arbitrator Warren sent us an Amended Final Decision and Award, dated July 11, 2014, covering the omitted issue, awarding us our fees, and inviting us to file an application for fees.

LRI has filed a petition in the Superior Court to vacate the Amended Final Decision and Award. We now need to respond by opposing LRI's petition to vacate.

Please draft for my review a brief in opposition to LRI's petition. Be guided by our Office Memorandum on Persuasive Briefs. You must be sure to refute each of the points raised in LRI's petition and argue persuasively why the court should deny LRI's petition.

MARTIN, RIVERA & TRAN, LLP

Attorneys and Counselors at Law

Eagle Point, Columbia

MEMORANDUM

August 15, 2011

SUBJECT: Persuasive Briefs

Unless otherwise instructed, attorneys shall include in all briefs a short and concise Statement of Facts written in such a way as to persuade the tribunal that the facts support our client's position.   The Statement of Facts is not an indiscriminate recitation of all the facts in the case.   Although the facts must be stated accurately, careful selection of the ones pertinent to the legal arguments and that support our client is not improper.

The Argument section of the brief should contain separate segments, each labeled with carefully crafted headings that summarize the argument in the ensuing segment.   Do not write a brief that contains only a single broad heading.   Each heading should succinctly state the reasons why the tribunal should adopt the position you are advocating and not merely a bare legal or factual proposition.

The body of each argument should match the relevant facts to the legal authorities and argue persuasively how the facts as applied to those authorities support our client's position.   Authority that favors our client should be emphasized, but contrary authority should be addressed in the argument and distinguished or explained.   Do not reserve argument for reply or supplemental briefs.

You need not prepare a table of contents, a table of cases, a summary of the argument, or an index.   These will be prepared after the draft is approved.

In the Matter of an Arbitration between RILEY INSTRUMENTS, INC., Plaintiff and LRI, INC., Defendant.	MAA Case No. 14-1322 **FINAL DECISION AND AWARD**
Including a counterclaim by LRI, Inc. for breach of contract to recover the contract price.	

I.

INTRODUCTION

Riley Instruments, Inc. (Riley) and LRI, Inc. (LRI) entered into a contract under which LRI agreed to manufacture and supply computer chips to Riley in accordance with Riley's specifications. This arbitration is pursuant to that contract, which provides, *inter alia*, that:

ARBITRATION OF DISPUTES.

In the event a dispute arises under this contract, which dispute the parties are unable to settle amicably, the parties agree that the dispute shall be submitted to final and binding arbitration to be conducted under the rules of the Manufacturers Arbitration Association. The arbitrator shall award a reasonable attorney's fee to the prevailing party in the dispute.

II.

THE ISSUES

At the commencement of the hearing in this matter, the parties agreed upon the following statement of the issues to be submitted to the Arbitrator for decision:

Whether LRI breached its contract by failing to manufacture the cp426i series chip according to Riley's specifications and whether LRI intentionally concealed a manufacturing flaw in the production run of the chips delivered to Riley. If so, what shall be the appropriate remedy? If not, shall LRI recover the contract price on its counterclaim?

III.

CONCLUSIONS AND AWARD

The Arbitrator finds and concludes that LRI breached its contract as alleged by Riley and that Riley suffered damages from said breach. According to the proof, Riley's damages, consisting of lost profits, cost of cover for replacement goods, delays in delivery of product to its customers, and associated administrative expenses, totaled $875,650.

Accordingly, the Arbitrator makes the following AWARD:

1. LRI shall forthwith pay Riley $875,650 as contract damages;
2. Said amount shall bear interest at the legal rate from and after the date of this AWARD;
3. LRI shall pay Riley $12,133 as its costs in this matter;
4. LRI shall pay $7,500 as administrative and filing fees to the Manufacturers Arbitration Association.
5. LRI shall take nothing on its counterclaim.

Dated: May 9, 2014

_____*Stanley Warren*_____

Stanley Warren
Arbitrator

MARTIN, RIVERA & TRAN, LLP

Attorneys and Counselors at Law

35 Birdshot Plaza, Suite 1900

Eagle Point, Columbia

May 27, 2014

Stanley Warren
Law Offices of Stanley Warren
4289 Greyfeather Drive, Suite 430
Eagle Point, Columbia

Re: Riley Instruments, Inc. v. LRI, Inc.
       Manufacturers Arbitration Association
       Case No. 14-1322

Dear Arbitrator Warren:

I write on behalf of my client, Riley Instruments, Inc. On May 12, 2014, we received your Final Decision and Award dated May 9, 2014. We wish to point out to you what we believe are inadvertent omissions therein, and we request that you change the Award to cover the omissions.

First: The agreed-upon submission stated two issues: (1) whether LRI breached its contract and (2) whether LRI intentionally concealed a manufacturing flaw. Regarding the second point, we refer you to our post-hearing brief in which we recite the following evidence, fully supported by the testimony and documents in the record:

LRI's former Director of Manufacturing gave unrebutted testimony that he knew about a flaw in the computer chips manufactured for Riley and that he consciously decided not to disclose it because he knew it would cause Riley to reject the chips. Also, we presented unrebutted evidence that Riley spent $75,000 for an engineering analysis to determine why the chips were not performing as intended and that it was only after incurring that expense that Riley discovered the flaw. In our brief, we also argued for an award of punitive damages based on LRI's intentional concealment.

Your Final Decision and Award does not appear to have dealt with the concealment issue and the damages attributable thereto, as well as the punitive damages remedy.

Second: The contract pursuant to which this arbitration was conducted provides that: "The arbitrator shall award a reasonable attorney's fee to the prevailing party in the dispute."

Although you did not explicitly state in your Award that Riley was the prevailing party, it is clear that Riley did prevail in all respects over LRI and is therefore entitled to its attorney's fee.

Accordingly, we respectfully request that you change your Final Decision and Award to cover the intentional concealment, punitive damages, and attorney's fee issues.

Very truly yours,

MARTIN, RIVERA & TRAN, LLP

By_____*Helen Rivera*_____

Helen Rivera, Partner

cc: Mark Stilton, Attorney for LRI, Inc.

LAW OFFICES OF MARK STILTON

MARK STILTON

Attorney at Law

1823 Herrick Blvd., Suite 3

Eagle Point, Columbia

May 30, 2014

Stanley Warren
Law Offices of Stanley Warren
4289 Greyfeather Drive, Suite 430
Eagle Point, Columbia

Re: <u>Riley Instruments, Inc. v. LRI, Inc.</u>
       Manufacturers Arbitration Association
       Case No. 14-1322

Dear Arbitrator Warren:

I strenuously object, on behalf of my client, LRI, Inc., to the request by Riley Instruments, Inc. that you amend your Final Decision and Award in the above-referenced matter. Suffice it to say that, having issued your *Final* Decision and Award, you are without authority, power, or jurisdiction by reason of the doctrine of *functus officio* to do anything further with respect to that Award.

Sincerely,

Mark Stilton

cc: Helen Rivera

ARBITRATION PROCEEDINGS BEFORE

THE MANUFACTURERS ARBITRATION ASSOCIATION

PURSUANT TO THE AGREEMENT OF THE PARTIES

In the Matter of an Arbitration between
 	
RILEY INSTRUMENTS, INC.,
 	
    Plaintiff
 	
and
 	
LRI, INC.,
 	
    Defendant.
	MAA Case No. 14-1322
	
	AMENDED
	FINAL DECISION
	AND AWARD

Including a counterclaim by LRI, Inc. for breach of contract to recover the contract price.	

I.

<u>INTRODUCTION</u>

On May 29, 2014, the Arbitrator received Riley Instruments, Inc.'s May 27, 2014 letter requesting an amended Final Decision and Award, asserting that the Arbitrator had inadvertently omitted from his May 9, 2014 Final Decision and Award rulings on three issues:

1. Whether LRI intentionally concealed a manufacturing defect and, if so, what damages Riley Instruments should recover as a consequence;

2. Whether Riley Instruments should recover punitive damages on account of the intentional concealment; and

3. Whether Riley Instruments should recover its attorney's fees.

LRI's attorney responded on May 30, 2014 in opposition to Riley's request by asserting that the Arbitrator is *functus officio* and therefore has no power to amend the initial Final Decision and Award.

II.

DISCUSSION

Counsel for Riley Instruments is correct in her assertion that the omissions recited in her May 27, 2014 letter were entirely inadvertent. The Arbitrator has reviewed the record in this case, including the transcript of the hearing, the documentary evidence, and the arguments set out in the post-hearing briefs of the parties and concludes that an Amended Final Decision and Award is appropriate and within the Arbitrator's power to resolve ambiguities and correct omissions.

First, the Arbitrator intended, but neglected, to state specifically that LRI intentionally concealed from Riley Instruments the manufacturing defect and, therefore breached the term in the contract between the parties that provided explicitly that, "LRI shall monitor the production of the cp426i series chip and furnish Riley with periodic quality control reports." Implicit in that term is LRI's obligation to inform Riley Instruments of any problems. The monetary award of $875,650 that was recited in the Arbitrator's May 9, 2014 Final Decision and Award in fact includes the $75,000 that Riley Instruments incurred for the engineering study that led to the discovery of the flaw. It should have been itemized as follows: $800,650 for lost profits, cost of cover for replacement goods, delays in delivery of product to its customers, and associated administrative expenses; $75,000 for the engineering study to discover the manufacturing flaw.

The record, by reason of the unrebutted testimony of the Director of Manufacturing formerly employed by LRI, also supports Riley Instruments' assertion that LRI's concealment was intentional and with knowledge that, if disclosed, it would have caused Riley Instruments to reject the entire production run of computer chips. (See transcript at p. 327.) The Arbitrator, again inadvertently, neglected to make that finding explicit in the original Final Decision and Award and hereby corrects that omission by making it explicit that LRI's concealment was intentional and with a motive to deceive. The Arbitrator finds he has the authority under the clear terms of the submission to determine the "appropriate remedy" and that LRI's intentional breach of contract warrants imposition of punitive damages to punish LRI for its unconscionable conduct. Accordingly, the Arbitrator awards $100,000 as punitive damages in favor of Riley Instruments and against LRI as prayed for in Riley Instruments' closing brief.

Finally, Riley Instruments is correct in its assertion that it is entitled to recover a reasonable attorney's fee in accordance with the arbitration provision of the parties' contract that states that "[t]he arbitrator shall award a reasonable attorney's fee to the prevailing party in the dispute." Obviously, Riley Instruments is the prevailing party. Thus, the Arbitrator hereby awards to Riley Instruments a reasonable attorney's fee.

III.
AMENDED AWARD

The Arbitrator incorporates herein by this reference his May 9, 2014 Final Decision and Award and issues the following AMENDED AWARD:

1. LRI shall forthwith pay Riley Instruments $800,650 as contract damages for lost profits, cost of cover for replacement goods, delays in delivery of product to its customers, and associated administrative expenses;

2. LRI shall forthwith pay Riley Instruments $75,000 as damages for the expense of an engineering study that led to the discovery of the manufacturing flaw;

3. LRI shall forthwith pay Riley Instruments $100,000 as punitive damages for the intentional concealment of the manufacturing flaw;

4. Said amounts shall bear interest at the legal rate from and after the date of this AMENDED AWARD;

5. LRI shall pay Riley $12,133 as its costs in this matter;

6. LRI shall pay $7,500 as administrative and filing fees to the Manufacturers Arbitration Association.

7. LRI shall take nothing on its counterclaim.

8. Riley Instruments, as the prevailing party in this dispute, shall recover a reasonable attorney's fee. Within 30 days of the date of this Amended Award, Riley Instruments shall lodge with the Arbitrator and serve upon LRI its application for attorney's fees, supported by billings and time records. Within 15 days thereafter, LRI shall lodge with the Arbitrator and serve upon Riley Instruments LRI's memorandum, if any, challenging Riley Instruments' application. The Arbitrator will then rule on the amount of fees based on the submissions of the parties.

Dated: July 11, 2014

_____*Stanley Warren*_____

Stanley Warren
Arbitrator

Mark Stilton
Law Offices of Mark Stilton
1823 Herrick Blvd., Suite 3
Eagle Point, Columbia

Attorney for LRI, Inc.

SUPERIOR COURT OF THE STATE OF COLUMBIA
RADLEY COUNTY

LRI, INC.,
 	
               Petitioner
 	
vs.
 	
RILEY INSTRUMENTS, INC.,
 	
               Respondent.
	Civ. Case No. 14-44378
	
	PETITION TO VACATE ARBITRATOR'S AMENDED FINAL DECISION AND AWARD

Including a counterclaim by LRI, Inc. for breach of contract to recover the contract price.	

     An arbitration was conducted under the rules of the Manufacturers Arbitration Association pursuant to a contract between LRI, Inc. and Riley Instruments, Inc. On May 9, 2014, Arbitrator Stanley Warren issued a *Final* Decision and Award in favor of Riley Instruments. On May 27, 2014, Riley Instruments, in a letter to the arbitrator, asserted that the arbitrator had failed to rule on certain issues and requested that the arbitrator amend the May 9, 2014 award to include the allegedly omitted issues.

     On July 11, 2014, Arbitrator Warren issued an Amended Final Decision and Award in which he purported to "correct" the earlier award. Both of the arbitrator's awards are attached hereto as exhibits.

LRI, Inc. moves on the following grounds to vacate the Amended Final Decision and Award.

1. Once he issued his Final Decision and Award, the arbitrator was *functus officio* and had no power whatsoever to amend or otherwise change the award. It is a fundamental common law principle that once an arbitrator has made and published an award, his authority is exhausted and he is *functus officio* and can do nothing more in regard to the subject matter of the arbitration. The policy that lies behind this is an unwillingness to permit one who is not a judicial officer, and who acts informally and sporadically, to reexamine a final decision that he has already rendered because of the potential evil of outside communication and unilateral influence which might affect a new conclusion. See, *Transport, Inc. v. National Petroleum Corp.*, Col. Ct. App. (1990).

2. The purported amendment and the request therefor were in any event untimely. Rule 46 of the Commercial Arbitration Rules of the Manufacturers Arbitration Association requires that the arbitrator must "dispose of the request [for a correction] within 20 days after service of the request." Also, Columbia Code of Procedure, Section 1284, requires that any request for a correction be made "not later than 10 days after service of a signed copy of the award on the applicant" and that the requested correction be made "not later than 30 days after service of a signed copy of the award on the applicant." On all counts, the requisite time limits were exceeded.

3. Both Rule 46 and the CCP Section 1286.6 allow the arbitrator to make "corrections" only for essentially clerical, typographical, or computational errors not affecting the merits of the award. The arbitrator clearly exceeded the scope of any power he may have had by (a) adding a finding, not made in the original award, regarding the alleged liability of LRI for an alleged intentional concealment, (b) recharacterizing the amount of the contract damages award, and (c) deciding that Riley Instruments is entitled to attorney's fees and claiming to retain the power to determine the amount. These are clearly substantive changes "affecting the merits of the award."

4. The arbitrator committed a grave error of law by awarding punitive damages in a contract case. It is a fundamental principle of law that punitive damages do not lie for breach of contract.

LRI, Inc. therefore moves the court to vacate the arbitrator's July 11, 2014 Amended Final Decision and Award.

Dated: July 16, 2014

Respectfully submitted,

LAW OFFICES OF MARK STILTON

By_____*Mark Stilton*_____

Mark Stilton
Attorney for LRI, Inc.

California
Bar
Examination

Performance Test B
LIBRARY

RILEY INSTRUMENTS, INC. v. LRI, INC.

LIBRARY

Commercial Arbitration Rules
Manufacturers Arbitration Association

Rule 43. Scope of Award

The arbitrator may grant any remedy or relief that the arbitrator deems just and equitable and within the scope of the agreement of the parties.

* * * * *

Rule 46. Modification of Award

Within 10 days after the service of an award, any party, upon notice to the other parties, may request the arbitrator to correct any clerical, typographical, or computational errors in the award. The arbitrator is not empowered to redetermine the merits of any claim already decided. The arbitrator shall dispose of the request within 20 days after service of the request to the arbitrator and any response thereto.

Columbia Arbitration Act
Columbia Code of Procedure (CCP)

Section 1283. Award

The award shall be in writing and signed by the arbitrators concurring therein. It shall include a determination of all the questions submitted to the arbitrators, the decision of which is necessary in order to determine the controversy.

Section 1284. Application for Correction

The arbitrators, upon written application of a party to the arbitration, may correct the award upon any of the grounds set forth in subdivisions (a) and (c) of Section 1286.6 not later than 30 days after service of a signed copy of the award on the applicant. Application for such correction shall be made not later than 10 days after service of a signed copy of the award on the applicant.

Section 1285. Petition to Confirm, Correct, or Vacate

Any party to an arbitration in which an award has been made may petition the court to confirm, correct or vacate the award. The petition shall name as respondents all parties to the arbitration and may name as respondents any other persons bound by the arbitration award.

* * * * *

Section 1285.2. Response to Petition

A response to a petition under this chapter may request the court to dismiss the petition or to confirm, correct or vacate the award.

* * * * *

Section 1286.2. Grounds for Vacation

The court shall vacate the award if the court determines any of the following:

(a) The award was procured by corruption, fraud or other undue means.

(b) There was corruption in any of the arbitrators.

(c) The rights of the party were substantially prejudiced by misconduct of a neutral arbitrator.

(d) The arbitrators exceeded their powers and the award cannot be corrected without affecting the merits of the decision upon the controversy submitted.

(e) The rights of the party were substantially prejudiced by the refusal of the arbitrators to postpone the hearing upon sufficient cause being shown therefor or by the refusal of the arbitrators to hear evidence material to the controversy or by other conduct of the arbitrators contrary to the provisions of this title.

* * * * *

Section 1286.6. Correction by Court

The court, unless it vacates the award pursuant to Section 1286.2, shall correct the award and confirm it as corrected if the court determines that:

    (a)   There was an evident miscalculation of figures or an evident mistake in the description of any person, thing or property referred to in the award;

    (b)   The arbitrators exceeded their powers but the award may be corrected without affecting the merits of the decision upon the controversy submitted; or

    (c)   The award is imperfect in a matter of form, not affecting the merits of the controversy.

Monroe v. Henson & Bailey

Columbia Supreme Court (1992)

Walter Monroe was employed as a lawyer by the law firm of Henson & Bailey under an employment contract that contained an agreement to submit "any dispute arising out of this contract to final and binding arbitration." There was a provision in the contract regarding allocation of attorney's fees in the event Monroe left the firm and took clients with him. When Monroe resigned, a number of clients followed him to his new practice, and a dispute arose over how to allocate the fees earned and to be earned. The parties submitted the dispute to an arbitrator, who essentially ruled against Monroe. Monroe petitioned the trial court to vacate the award. That court denied his petition.

We granted review and directed the parties to address the limited issue of whether and under what conditions a trial court may review an arbitrator's decision.

1. *The General Rule of Arbitral Finality*.

This case involves private, nonjudicial arbitration, which the parties submitted to an arbitrator pursuant to their written agreement. The Columbia Arbitration Act, found in the Code of Procedure (CCP), represents a comprehensive statutory scheme regulating private arbitration in this state and expresses a strong public policy in favor of arbitration as a speedy and relatively inexpensive means of dispute resolution.

The arbitration clause included in the employment agreement in this case specifically states that the arbitrator's decision would be both binding and final. The arbitrator's decision should be the end, not the beginning, of the dispute. Thus, an arbitration decision is final and conclusive *because the parties have agreed that it be so.* The courts simply assure that the parties receive the benefit of that bargain by minimizing judicial intervention in the arbitration process.

Arbitrators may base their decisions upon broad principles of justice and equity, and in doing so may expressly or impliedly reject a claim that a party might successfully have asserted in a judicial action. Moreover, they are not bound to award on principles of dry law, but may decide on principles of equity and good conscience, and make their award according to what is just and good. Thus, it is the general rule that, with narrow exceptions, an arbitrator's decision cannot be reviewed for errors of fact or law.

In reaffirming this general rule, we recognize there is a risk that the arbitrator will make a mistake. That risk, however, is acceptable – first, because the parties have voluntarily and contractually agreed to bear that risk, and second, because by enacting the Columbia Arbitration Act, the Legislature has reduced the risk by providing for judicial review in circumstances involving serious problems with the award itself or with the fairness of the arbitration process. The Act sets forth the grounds for both vacation and correction of an award. See, CCP Sections 1286.2 and 1286.6.

In the present case, Monroe puts forth three exceptions to the general rule that he claims apply to his case. First, he claims a court may review an arbitrator's decision if an error of law is apparent on the face of the award and that error causes substantial injustice. Second, he claims the arbitrator exceeded his powers. Third, he argues courts will not enforce arbitration decisions that are illegal or violate public policy.

2. *Error of Law on the Face of the Arbitration Decision Does Not Warrant Judicial Review*.

As previously noted, the Legislature has set forth grounds for vacation and correction of an arbitration award, and an error of law is not one of the grounds.

Early cases, predating the Columbia Arbitration Act, followed the common law rule that arbitration awards were freely reviewable by the courts, particularly if the challenge to the award was based on an error of law. Later cases drew back on that view, especially in light of the passage of the Act, but even then the courts were reluctant to adopt a hands-off approach. Finally, this court pronounced that the merits of the controversy between the parties are not subject to judicial review. The form and sufficiency of the evidence and the credibility and good faith of the parties, in the absence of corruption, fraud or undue means in obtaining an award, are not matters for judicial review. In this way, this court suggested that the Columbia Arbitration Act – and not the common law – established the limits of judicial review of arbitration awards. Thus, we held that in the absence of some limiting clause in the arbitration agreement, the merits of the award, either on questions of fact or of law, *may not be reviewed except as provided in the statute.*

The law has thus evolved from its common law origins and moved toward a more clearly delineated scheme rooted in statute. We adhere to the line of cases that limit judicial review of private arbitration awards to those cases in which there exists a statutory ground to vacate or correct the award. Those decisions permitting review of an award where an error of law appears on the face of the award causing substantial injustice have perpetuated a point of view that is inconsistent with the modern view of private arbitration and are therefore disapproved.

3. *The Arbitrator Did Not Exceed His Powers*.

Monroe argues that, in allocating the earned and to-be-earned fees as he did, the arbitrator exceeded his powers, but it is unclear what Monroe's theory is other than that the arbitrator's interpretation of the contract is erroneous. It is well settled that arbitrators do not exceed their powers merely because they assign an erroneous reason for their decision. A contrary holding would permit the exception to swallow the rule of limited judicial review; a litigant could always contend the arbitrator erred and thus exceeded his powers. To the extent Monroe argues his case comes within CCP Section 1286.2, subdivision (d), merely because the arbitrator reached an erroneous decision, we reject the point.

It is within the "powers" of the arbitrator to resolve the entire "merits" of the "controversy submitted" by the parties. Obviously, the "merits" include all the contested issues of law and fact submitted to the arbitrator for decision. The arbitrator's resolution of these issues is what the parties bargained for in the arbitration agreement. Monroe does not argue that the arbitrator's award strayed beyond the scope of the parties' agreement by resolving issues the parties did not agree to arbitrate. The agreement to arbitrate encompassed "any dispute arising out of" the employment contract. The parties' dispute over the allocation of attorney's fees following termination of employment clearly arose out of the employment contract; the arbitrator's award does no more than resolve that dispute. Under these circumstances, the arbitrator was within his "powers" in resolving the questions of law presented to him.

A related paramount principle that bears on the arbitrator's power to determine and resolve the merits is this: Unless the contract, the submission, or the rules governing the arbitration provide otherwise, an arbitrator's choice of relief awarded to the prevailing party does not exceed his or her powers so long as it bears a rational relationship to the underlying contract and to the breach thereof *as interpreted, expressly or impliedly, by the arbitrator.* This holds true as to any plausible theory of the arbitrator's interpretation of the contract. In this case, the logical connection of the nature of the relief fashioned by the arbitrator to the underlying contract is plain. Thus, the award is not subject to vacation or correction based on any of the statutory grounds asserted by Monroe.

We conclude that an award reached by an arbitrator pursuant to a contractual agreement to arbitrate is not subject to judicial review except on the grounds set forth in CCP Sections 1286.2 and 1286.6. Further, the existence of an error of law apparent on the face of the award, even one that causes substantial injustice, does not provide grounds for judicial review.

The judgment is affirmed.

Marco v. Chandler
Columbia Court of Appeals (1995)

Plaintiffs and appellants Joel Marco and Linda Marco (collectively, Marco) appeal a judgment insofar as it awards $19,575 in attorney's fees to defendant and respondent Dixie N. Chandler (Chandler). The essential issues are whether the arbitrator exceeded his powers by denying an award of attorney's fees to Chandler, and whether the trial court erred in awarding attorney's fees to Chandler for the underlying arbitration instead of remanding to the arbitrator for that purpose.

In March 1991, Marco entered into a real estate purchase contract to acquire certain property from Chandler. Marco subsequently filed an action for rescission. Because the contract contained an arbitration clause, the matter was referred to the Manufacturers Arbitration Association. In an award made January 9, 1992, the arbitrator denied Marco's claim against Chandler and denied all requests for attorney's fees. On April 20, 1992, Chandler filed a petition in the trial court to correct the arbitration award. Chandler contended that the arbitrator exceeded his power by not applying the attorney's fee provision and that the error appeared on the face of the record. The contract between the parties provided that "[i]n any action, proceeding or arbitration arising out of this agreement, the prevailing party shall be entitled to reasonable attorney's fees." The matter was heard May 22, 1992, at which time the trial court ordered the matter back to the arbitrator to clarify his denial of attorney's fees to Chandler.

On October 13, 1992, the arbitrator filed a clarification of the award, stating that Chandler prevailed against Marco but that, in rendering the award, he believed he had the discretion to deny the request for attorney's fees, notwithstanding the determination that Chandler was the prevailing party. He added, "If the arbitrator does not have that discretion and the prevailing parties are entitled to attorney's fees as a matter of right, attorneys' fees should be awarded to the prevailing parties to the degree such fees were incurred in arbitrating the claim upon which they prevailed."

On November 20, 1992, Chandler filed a second petition in the trial court to correct and to affirm the award as clarified by the arbitrator. In the petition, Chandler sought a correction of the award to reflect her entitlement to reasonable attorney's fees as the prevailing party. Marco filed opposition papers, arguing that the petition was time-barred, that the trial court lacked the power to correct the award even if the petition were timely, that Chandler had failed to provide any admissible and competent evidence of whether the attorney's fees sought were reasonable or necessary, and that sanctions should be imposed against Chandler and her counsel.

Chandler's reply papers asserted the petition was timely. Chandler's counsel attached a copy of her prior bill in this matter, in the amount of $19,575, and asked the court to make a determination of the *amount* of fees Chandler was entitled to.

The trial court granted Chandler's motion and awarded Chandler $19,575 as a reasonable attorney's fee. Marco appealed.

1. *There is no merit to Marco's contention that the trial court was bound by the arbitrator's denial of an award of attorney's fees.*

Marco, citing the Columbia Supreme Court's decision in *Monroe v. Henson & Bailey*, contends the trial court was bound by the arbitrator's decision denying Chandler an award of attorney's fees, i.e., that the trial court had no power to review the arbitrator's decision. The argument lacks merit.

In *Monroe*, the Supreme Court clarified the law as to the limited scope of judicial review of arbitration awards. *Monroe* held an award rendered by an arbitrator pursuant to a contractual agreement to arbitrate is not subject to judicial review except on the grounds set forth in the Columbia Arbitration Act.

Here, the arbitrator's decision to deny Chandler an award of attorney's fees, notwithstanding his finding Chandler was the prevailing party, exceeded his powers because the agreement provides that "the prevailing party *shall* be entitled to reasonable attorney's fees." (Italics added.)

Had the arbitrator found neither Marco nor Chandler was the prevailing party, the arbitrator properly could have declined to make any award of attorney's fees. But having made a finding Chandler was the prevailing party, the arbitrator was compelled by the terms of the agreement to award her reasonable attorney's fees and costs. That error was subject to correction because Section 1286.6(b) of the Columbia Arbitration

Act provides an award shall be corrected if "[*t*]*he arbitrators exceeded their powers* [and] *the award may be corrected without affecting the merits of the decision ....*" (Italics added.)

2. *There is, however, merit to Marco's contention that the amount of attorney's fees to be awarded for the arbitration proceeding is to be determined by the arbitrator.*

The issue is whether the arbitrator should have been directed to decide the *amount* of attorney's fees to be awarded for the arbitration proceeding, or whether the issue of the amount of those fees was a matter for the trial court.

An award of attorney fees for the arbitration itself is within the arbitrator's purview. After the arbitrator declined to award Chandler her attorney's fees, notwithstanding his determination she was the prevailing party, the trial court was empowered to correct the award to provide for an award of attorney's fees to Chandler. However, the trial court should have remanded the matter to the arbitrator to determine the *amount* of attorney's fees to which Chandler was entitled for the arbitration proceeding, rather than making that determination at the trial court level. It is the arbitrator, not the trial court, who is best situated to determine the amount of reasonable attorney's fees to be awarded for the conduct of the arbitration proceeding. We remind the arbitrator that he is compelled by the parties' agreement to award reasonable attorney's fees to the prevailing party and that he lacks discretion to do otherwise.

The judgment is reversed insofar as it awards $19,575 in attorney's fees to Chandler, and the matter is remanded to the arbitrator for a determination of the amount of attorney's fees.

Transport, Inc. v. National Petroleum Corp.
Columbia Court of Appeals (1990)

This case involves an arbitration of a dispute between the petitioner, Transport, Inc. (Transport), and the respondent, National Petroleum Corp. (NPC), over the transportation of petroleum products. The issues that the parties initially submitted to the arbitrators for decision were: (1) whether NPC breached its contract by canceling the fourth shipment it had agreed to tender to Transport, and (2) if so, what damages Transport suffered. At the commencement of the arbitration, the parties agreed to bifurcate the liability and damages issues, requesting the arbitrators to issue first a "partial final award" on the question of liability, i.e., whether NPC breached the contract.

After issuance of a "partial final award" in which the panel of arbitrators found in favor of Transport on the issue of liability, one of the three arbitrators died. Transport sought in the court below to confirm the "partial final award" and requested the court to appoint a replacement for the deceased arbitrator and remand the matter to the reconstituted panel for a decision on the issue of damages.

NPC cross-petitioned the court to vacate the partial final award, require the parties to select a new panel of arbitrators, and commence the matter anew. The court below, exercising its authority under the Columbia Arbitration Act, appointed an arbitrator to replace the deceased one, confirmed the partial final award, and remanded the case to the reconstituted panel for decision on the issue of damages.

On this appeal, NPC argues that, notwithstanding that the ruling of the arbitrators here was titled "partial *final* award," the general rule is that an arbitral decision is not final unless it conclusively decides every point required by and included in the submission of the parties. That is in fact the general rule, but it must be assessed in light of two other pertinent principles: First, if the parties agree that the panel of arbitrators is to make a final decision as to part of the dispute, the arbitrators have the authority and responsibility to do so. Second, once the arbitrators have finally decided the submitted issues, they are in common law parlance *functus officio*, meaning that their authority over those questions is ended.

The latter principles govern the present dispute. The parties agreed at the commencement of the arbitration to a bifurcated decision. They asked the panel to decide the issue of liability. Prior to the death of the third arbitrator, the panel ruled on that issue conclusively, deciding every point required by and included in the first part of the parties' submission. Thus, with respect to liability, the original panel was *functus officio*, so the reconstituted panel cannot be ordered to rearbitrate that issue.

The Columbia Arbitration Act makes specific provision for filling vacancies in arbitration panels: The court is authorized to do so upon application of a party if the agreement of the parties does not otherwise provide. This authority extends to pending arbitrations. The court below acted within its authority.

We affirm the judgment of the court below.

Classic Construction, Inc. v. Vladomir Development Co., et al.
Columbia Court of Appeals (1999)

Appellants Vladomir Development Company (Vladomir) and Mandeville Township (Mandeville) appeal from a judgment confirming an amended arbitration award in favor of respondent Classic Construction, Inc. (Classic). Vladomir and Mandeville contend that the arbitrator exceeded his powers by amending the award to determine an issue he had failed initially to decide. They contend that the trial court was required to vacate the amended award and order the entire dispute reheard by a new arbitrator.

Facts and Procedural Background

Classic, a subcontractor, performed asphalt work and other improvements for Vladomir at an elementary school in Mandeville. A dispute arose about the work. Classic stopped work and served a stop payment notice upon Mandeville, i.e., a notice that Mandeville should withhold payment pending settlement of the dispute. Classic then sued Vladomir and Mandeville for damages.

The parties stipulated that the entire dispute would be resolved by binding arbitration. They briefed the questions presented and introduced oral and documentary evidence on all issues. The parties each submitted proposed forms of judgment that addressed all the questions submitted to the arbitrator. The arbitrator issued his decision awarding Classic $42,051 in damages against Vladomir for breach of contract, but the award did not resolve the claim against Mandeville based upon the stop payment notice. The arbitrator did not, therefore, determine all the questions submitted.

After receiving the award, counsel for Classic wrote a letter to the arbitrator requesting that he amend the award to include a judgment against Mandeville based upon the stop payment notice. Counsel for Classic did not send a copy of this letter to the attorney representing both Vladomir and Mandeville.

Four days later, counsel for Classic telephoned the administrator for the arbitrator. The arbitrator confirmed that he had received the letter and said he would make a decision in the next few days. These calls were also ex parte.

The arbitrator thereafter issued an amended award, which included a finding favorable to Classic on the cause of action against Mandeville. The amended portion of the award provided: "Classic's stop notice directed to Mandeville is found valid for purposes of this action." Upon receipt of the amended award, counsel for Vladomir and Mandeville attempted unsuccessfully to contact the arbitrator and then learned of the ex parte communications from counsel for Classic.

Classic subsequently petitioned the trial court to confirm the amended arbitration award. Vladomir and Mandeville opposed the petition, moved to vacate the amended award, and requested that the trial court order that the entire dispute be reheard by a new arbitrator. In a declaration submitted to the trial court, the arbitrator confirmed that the parties had submitted proposed judgments at the conclusion of the arbitration that resolved the causes of action based upon the contract and the stop payment notice. The arbitrator further confirmed that counsel for Classic notified him that the award omitted a finding on the latter cause of action, and that he advised counsel for Classic that he had all the information necessary from the documents received at the arbitration and his notes to render a decision on this cause of action. The arbitrator stated that his failure to address the stop notice claim was inadvertent.

The trial court declined to vacate the amended award, granted Classic's petition to confirm the amended award, and entered judgment in favor of Classic for $42,051 and against both Vladomir and Mandeville.

Discussion

Vladomir and Mandeville contend that the trial court erred in refusing to vacate the amended arbitration award because the arbitrator: (1) exceeded his power under CCP Section 1284 by amending the award; (2) violated procedural requirements for amending or correcting the award under Section 1284; (3) issued an amended award based upon information obtained outside the arbitration in violation of CCP Section 1282.2; and (4) engaged in misconduct with Classic's counsel in violation of CCP Sections 1286.2 and 1286.6. We disagree.

As a general rule, courts will indulge every reasonable intendment to give effect to arbitration proceedings. To ensure that an arbitrator's decision is the end of the dispute, arbitration awards are subject to very narrow judicial review. See, *Monroe v. Henson & Bailey*, Columbia Supreme Court (1992).

Arbitrators must produce an award that includes "a determination of all the questions submitted to the arbitrators, the decision of which is necessary in order to determine the controversy." (CCP Section 1283.) The consequence of an omission to decide all the questions is not addressed by Section 1283 or by any other provisions of the Act. Nothing in the statutory scheme either authorizes or prohibits the amendment of an award.

Section 1286.2 sets forth the exclusive grounds for vacating an arbitration award. Except on these grounds, arbitration awards are immune from judicial review in proceedings to confirm or challenge the award. (*Monroe, supra.*)

The record here does not establish that the amended arbitration award was procured by corruption, undue means, or misconduct of the arbitrator. In a sworn declaration, the arbitrator explained that he inadvertently had not resolved one cause of action and that, when contacted by Classic's counsel, he informed counsel that he had all the information from the documents admitted during the arbitration and his notes to issue a decision on the omitted claim. Thus, the record does not reveal that the arbitrator considered information outside the arbitration proceeding in ruling upon the claim. Nor does the record reveal any improper intent or attempt to influence the arbitrator on the part of opposing counsel. Classic's counsel explained, in a declaration submitted under penalty of perjury, that he had no intent to reargue the matters presented at the arbitration or bias the arbitrator, but intended only to remind the arbitrator that both sides had desired a ruling on the claim and had included it in proposed judgments previously submitted to him.

In the absence of a showing that the arbitrator was improperly influenced or actually considered evidence outside the original arbitration proceedings such that appellants needed a further opportunity to be heard on the stop notice claim, appellants cannot demonstrate that the amended award was procured by corruption, fraud, undue means, or misconduct of the arbitrator within the meaning of Section 1286.2.

The remaining issue is whether issuance of the amended award in response to an ex parte communication is an action in excess of the arbitrator's powers or constitutes "other conduct ... contrary to the provisions" of the Act. We conclude that it is not.

Section 1284 authorizes an arbitrator, upon written application of a party to the arbitration, to *correct* the award upon either of the grounds set forth in Section 1286.6, subdivisions (a) and (c), i.e., where there is a miscalculation of amounts, a mistake in the description of a person or property referred to in the award, or where there is a defect *in the form* of the award that does not affect the merits of the controversy. Any application to correct an arbitration award under this section requires notice to the opposing party.

The *amendment* of the arbitration award in this case does not fall within these subdivisions. The arbitrator was not "correcting" a miscalculation or description contained in the prior award or correcting a defect in its "form." Rather, he was resolving the remainder of the dispute submitted to him. Thus, the time limits specified in Section 1284 do not apply.

The absence of a statutory provision authorizing amendment of an award does not deprive the arbitrator of jurisdiction to do so. The parties concede that the arbitrator had authority to decide the entire dispute, including the cause of action against Mandeville. The stop notice claim was raised in the pleadings, briefed by the parties, and included in proposed judgments submitted by both sides to the arbitrator. The amendment was made promptly. It is not inconsistent with other provisions of the original award and it does not substantially prejudice the legitimate interests of any party. In our view, the arbitrator was simply finishing his assignment by making a complete and full award on the matters submitted to him for resolution.

It has been suggested that the ancient rule of *functus officio* requires the award to be vacated under the circumstances we face here. That rule survives, but just barely, to bar arbitrators from revisiting and changing *complete* awards, i.e., awards where they in fact decided all the issues presented to them. But cases holding that an *incomplete* award is a nullity and must be vacated were generally decided before Columbia's Arbitration Act and the Supreme Court's instruction that the courts indulge every reasonable intendment to give effect to arbitration proceedings. To deny arbitrators the authority to complete their task under such circumstances elevates form over substance.

We conclude Columbia's contractual arbitration law permits arbitrators to issue an amended award to resolve an issue omitted from the original award through the mistake, inadvertence, or excusable neglect of the arbitrator if the amendment is made before judicial confirmation of the original award, is not inconsistent with other findings on the merits of the controversy, and does not cause demonstrable prejudice to the legitimate interests of any party.

This opinion should not be read to condone the actions of Classic's counsel in communicating ex parte with the arbitrator. Counsel's ex parte communications were inappropriate, and under different, more egregious circumstances, might require vacation of an arbitration award.

The judgment is affirmed.

PT-B: SELECTED ANSWER 1

STATEMENT OF FACTS

LRI, Inc. (LRI) willfully and deceptively breached a contract with Riley Instruments, Inc. (Riley), under which LRI agreed to manufacture and supply computer chips to Riley in accordance with Riley's specifications. The contract provided for "final and binding arbitration [of disputes] to be conducted under the rules of the Manufacturers Arbitration Association." The contract further provided that "[t]he arbitrator shall award a reasonable attorney's fee to the prevailing party in the dispute" (emphasis added).

At arbitration, the parties agreed to the following statement of issues: "Whether LRI breached its contract by failing to manufacture the cp426i series chip according to Riley's specifications and whether LRI concealed a manufacturing flaw in the production run of the chips delivered by Riley. If so, what shall be the appropriate remedy? If no, shall LRI recover the contract price on its counterclaim?"

Prior to the arbitrator's May 9, 2014 Final Decision and Award (FD&A), Riley presented evidence of LRI's intentional concealment of the flaw, Riley's engineering analysis to determine the flaw (costing $75,000), and the appropriateness of punitive damages based on LRI's intentional misconduct. In its FD&A, the arbitrator concluded that LRI breached its contract. It awarded $875,650 in contract damages, post-judgment interest, $12,133 in costs, and $7,500 in administrative and filing fees against LRI. However, the FD&A failed to decide the issues of intentional concealment and punitive damages. Furthermore, it failed to explicitly declare a prevailing party—which clearly was Riley—or award a reasonable attorney's fee.

On May 27, 2014, counsel for Riley wrote a letter to the arbitrator bringing these omissions to his attention. A copy of the letter was sent to counsel for LRI. On May 30, 2014, counsel for LRI wrote in opposition to amending the FD&A.

The arbitrator completed his original obligations by publishing an Amended FD&A on July 11, 2014. The Amended FD&A clarified that LRI was guilty of intentional concealment, that Riley was the prevailing party, that punitive damages were appropriate, and that LRI shall pay Riley's attorney's fee.

LRI petitioned to vacate the Amended FD&A on July 16, 2014. Riley now submits this Brief in Opposition.

ARGUMENT

I. The Arbitrator Had Power to Amend the Final Decision and Award Because He Failed to Make a Complete Award and Thus Failed to Fulfill His Original Obligations

"[T]he general rule is that an arbitral decision is not final unless it conclusively decides every point required by and included in the submission of the parties." (Transport, Inc. v. Nat'l Petroleum Corp.) "Columbia's contractual arbitration law permits arbitrators to issue an amended award to resolve an issue omitted from the original award through the mistake, inadvertence, or excusable neglect of the arbitrator if the amendment is made before judicial confirmation of the original award, is not inconsistent with other findings on the merits of the controversy, and does not cause demonstrable prejudice to the legitimate interests of any party." (Classic Construction, Inc. v. Vladomir Development Co.) This is precisely the situation of this case: the arbitrator failed to resolve an issue, the omission of which he called "entirely inadvertent." (Amended FD&A.) Therefore, the decision was not final, because it failed to "conclusively decide every point required by and included in the submission of the parties." (See Transport.)

Nonetheless, LRI claims that "the arbitrator was functus officio and had no power whatsoever to amend or otherwise change the award." (Petition to Vacate.) Not so. It improperly relies on Transport, which is inapposite to the facts at hand. Transport held that there were two principles that limited an arbitrator's ability to amend an award. "First, if the parties agree that the panel of arbitrators is to make a final decision as to part of the dispute, the arbitrators have the authority and responsibility to do so. Second, once the arbitrators have finally decided the submitted issues, they are in common law parlance functus officio." (Transport.) In that case, an arbitrator died after deciding only part of the issues. Crucially, however, the parties had agreed prior to arbitration to bifurcate the issues instead of having them decided all at once. Because the parties made such an agreement, and one bifurcated issue was finally decided, it could not be amended.

This case is easily distinguishable from Transport. Here, the parties did not agree to bifurcate the issues. Instead, they submitted all issues, which are greatly intertwined, to the arbitrator for simultaneous decision. There is no indication that either party desired the issues to be individually decided, and there is certainly no agreement to that effect. Therefore, the arbitrator had not "finally decided" the issues submitted, and he was free to amend his inadvertent omissions.

In any event, the rule of functus officio "survives, but just barely." (Classic Construction.) Early cases, prior to Columbia's Arbitration Act, held that incomplete awards could not be amended. (Id.) However, "[t]o deny arbitrators the authority to complete their task under such circumstances elevates form over substance." (Id.) Instead, Classic Construction unequivocally holds that the doctrine of functus officio does not bar the amendment of incomplete awards when the omission is due to "mistake, inadvertence, or excusable neglect." (Id.). Because the arbitrator's omission was through inadvertence in this case, he is not barred by any "barely surviving" rule.

Functus Officio does not apply to these facts; therefore, the arbitrator had power to amend the FD&A.

II. The Amendment and Request Therefor Were Timely, Because Neither Rule 46 Nor CCP § 1284 Applies to a Correction of an Inadvertent Omission

a. The Amendment Is Not Time-Barred By Rule 46

Rule 46 of Commercial Arbitration governs the modifications of awards. It prevents the arbitrator from "redetermin[ing] the merits of any claim already decided" but allows the arbitrator "to correct any clerical, typographical, or computational errors in the award." (Rule 46.) A party must request such a correction within 10 days of service of the award. LRI claims that Rule 46 bars amendment. If Rule 46 applied, that would be true, because Riley received the FD&A on May 12, 2014 and requested correction on May 27, 2014. However, as explained below, Rule 46 is inapplicable to these facts.

Riley did not request a correction of a clerical, typographical, or computational error in the FD&A. It requested instead that the arbitrator complete his original duties set forth in the contract between LRI and Riley, and those set forth in the arbitration proceedings. The thrust of the current dispute is not in the merits of the case, or in the typography of the original FD&A. Instead, the dispute is over the fact that the arbitrator made omissions of duties he was legally obligated to complete, not typographical mistakes. Because the relief Riley requested in its May 27, 2014 letter does not fall within the purview of Rule 46, it is not constrained by the time limits in Rule 46.

b. The Amendment Is Not Time-Barred By CCP § 1284

CCP § 1284 allows corrections to an arbitration award, if upon grounds set forth in § 1286.6(a) and (c), as long as application for correction is "made not later than 10 days after service of a signed copy of the award on the applicant." (CCP § 1284.) LRI incorrectly claims that Riley is constrained by § 1284's 10-day time limit.

Classic Construction controls this issue. The court there held, "The amendment of the arbitration award in this case does not fall within [§ 1284]. The arbitrator was not 'correcting' a miscalculation or description contained in the prior award or correcting a defect in its 'form.' Rather, he was resolving the remainder of the dispute submitted to him. Thus, the time limits specified in Section 1283 do not apply." (Classic Construction.) In Classic Construction, the arbitrator did not resolve certain claims that were brought before it. (Id.) This failure was brought to the arbitrator's attention by counsel for one of the parties in ex parte proceedings. (Id.) The arbitrator issued an amended award, making a favorable finding on the originally omitted issue for the party that brought the omission to his attention. (Id.) The arbitrator stated his failure to address the omitted claim was inadvertent. (Id.) In the subsequent appeal from the amendment, the court held that because the arbitrator was obligated under CCP § 1283 to make a determination on all questions submitted to it, and because his failure was inadvertent, amendment was proper. (Id.) It further held that, while not condoning ex parte proceedings, there was no evidence of corruption, fraud, or undue means. (Id.) Therefore, the amendment was valid, notwithstanding § 1284's time limit.

This case is highly analogous. The parties briefed and presented evidence on several issues that the arbitrator did not address in his original FD&A. Later, Riley brought these omissions to the arbitrator's attention in a letter that was also sent to opposing counsel. As in Classic Construction, the arbitrator admitted that the omissions were "entirely inadvertent." He then issued an Amended FD&A that corrected these omissions without any substantive changes to the underlying merits of the case. Importantly, every single issue the arbitrator clarified in his Amended FD&A had previously been argued prior to the original FD&A.

In sum, Classic Construction clearly holds that § 1284's time limit is inapplicable to the facts of this case. Therefore, Riley's letter and the subsequent corrections in the Amended FD&A were timely.

III. The Arbitrator Made a Proper Correction Because Fulfilling His Original Obligations Was Not Beyond the Scope of His Power

    a. The Columbia Arbitration Act Does Not Preclude Amendment

"Arbitrators must produce an award that includes 'a determination of all the questions submitted to the arbitrators, the decision of which is necessary in order to determine the controversy.'" (Classic Construction (quoting CCP § 1283) (emphasis in original).) "The consequence of an omission to decide all the questions is not addressed by Section 1283 or by any other provision of the Act. Nothing in the statutory scheme either authorizes or prohibits the amendment of an award." (Id.)

In this case, the arbitrator's original FD&A failed to "include a determination of all the questions submitted" to him. This is a clear violation of CCP § 1283—a violation that Classic Construction holds is not beyond the arbitrator's power of amendment. LRI claims that the arbitrator exceeded the scope of his power in three ways. However, in each instance, the arbitrator clearly had the power to correct his omissions.

b. The Arbitrator Had the Power to Clarify that LRI was Liable for Intentional Concealment

The arbitrator was clearly entitled to clarify that LRI was liable for intentional concealment because this is one of the explicit issues the parties presented in arbitration. (See FD&A Issue Statement ("[W]hether LRI intentionally concealed a manufacturing flaw in the production run of the chips delivered to Riley").) CCP § 1283 requires the arbitrator to determine all questions submitted to him. If he fails to do so, nothing in the statutory scheme prevents him from amending the award. (See Classic Construction.) Here, the arbitrator inadvertently omitted the decision on this issue and subsequently corrected his mistake. Doing so was entirely proper—indeed, it was mandated by § 1283. LRI cannot now claim the arbitrator does not have the power to decide an issue it agreed to present to the arbitrator. The issue should have been in the original FD&A, and § 1283 allows it to be in the Amended FD&A.

c. The Arbitrator Had the Power to Recharacterize the Amount of the Contract Damages Award

LRI claims that the arbitrator should not have recharacterized the amount of the contract damages award. LRI is wrong. The arbitrator was justified in correcting the amount of the award based on his clarification that LRI was guilty of intentional concealment. "The Arbitrator intended, but neglected to state specifically that LRI intentionally concealed . . . ." (Amended FD&A.) The monetary award of $875,650 recited in the original FD&A was based on this negligent omission to specify that "LRI's concealment was intentional and with a motive to deceive." (Id.)

Even if the ability to correct the contract damages amount was not implicit in clarifying his finding, the arbitrator was justified in his recharacterization under CCP § 1286.6(a). This allows for the correction of an award "if the court determines that there was an evident miscalculation of figures." Under Classic Construction, as discussed above, the 10-day time limit of § 1284 does not apply when the arbitrator is "resolving the remainder of the dispute submitted to him." That is precisely what the arbitrator did here. His actions were proper because the original contract damages amount was based on an incomplete finding. Furthermore, LRI will not suffer any prejudice based on this amount, because it totals the exact same number. The arbitrator merely clarified where $75,000 of those contract damages came from. At the end of the day, LRI will pay the exact same amount in contract damages.

d. The Arbitrator Had the Power to Decide that Riley was Entitled to Attorney's Fees and to Retain the Power to Determine the Amount

It is clear Riley was the prevailing party in this arbitration. (See Amended FD&A ("Obviously, Riley Instruments is the prevailing party.").) The contract between Riley and LRI stated that the "arbitrator shall award a reasonable attorney's fee to the prevailing party in the dispute" (emphasis added). The word "shall" leaves no discretion to the arbitrator; he must award attorney's fees after making a determination of a prevailing party. The contract in effect bound the arbitrator to make two decisions: (1)

who the prevailing party was; and (2) how much to award in fees. Again, the omission to do so in the original FD&A does not preclude a clarification in the Amended FD&A.

This case is analogous to Marco v. Chandler. The parties in that case also went to arbitration under a contract that stated that "the prevailing party shall be entitled to reasonable attorney's fees." (Marco.) The arbitrator in Marco declined to award the prevailing party—Chandler—attorney's fees. (Id.) The court held that by doing so, the arbitrator "exceeded his powers because the agreement provides that 'the prevailing party shall be entitled to reasonable attorney's fees.'" (Id.)

Based on Marco, LRI's argument flies in the face of prevailing law. It is not that the arbitrator in this case exceeded his powers by amending the FD&A to include an attorney's fee award; he would have exceeded his powers by not doing so. As Marco held, he "lacks the discretion to do otherwise." (Id.) Riley and LRI explicitly agreed that the prevailing party in arbitration would be entitled to reasonable attorney's fees. LRI cannot in good faith dispute the fact that Riley prevailed in this arbitration, and it has no legal basis to escape its contractual obligation to pay Riley's attorney's fees.

Furthermore, the arbitrator is entitled to determine the amount of attorney's fees. Under Marco, the decision of the amount of fees lies with the arbitrator. (See id. ("It is the arbitrator, not the trial court, who is best situated to determine the amount of reasonable attorney's fees to be awarded for the conduct of the arbitration proceeding.").) As in Marco, the arbitrator properly withheld the power to determine the amount of reasonable fees.

IV. Punitive Damages Were Appropriate Because LRI Willfully Deceived Riley; In Any Event, This Court Has No Power to Vacate or Correct the Award Because Neither CCP §§ 1286.2 Nor 1286.6 Applies

LRI, without one scintilla of legal support, claims that the "arbitrator committed a grave error of law by awarding punitive damages in a contract case." As explained below, the arbitrator was wholly justified in awarding punitive damages for willful intent to deceive. Even if there were an error of law, however, the award must still stand.

a. The Arbitrator Was Justified In Awarding Punitive Damages

The arbitrator awarded "$100,000 as punitive damages for the intentional concealment of the manufacturing flaw." (Amended FD&A.) It found that the concealment occurred "with a motive to deceive." (Id.) The parties agreed that the arbitrator shall determine the appropriate remedy. (See FD&A.) This includes, the arbitrator held, an award of punitive damages. Although under contract law, punitive damages are not generally awarded, it is clear that they can be properly awarded in instances of intentional deceit. The arbitrator found such intentional deception in this case; as such, he did not make an error of law. Certainly, any decision here cannot be described, as LRI baldly asserts, as a "grave error of law." Quite the contrary: LRI engaged in grave deception, and now it does not want to pay the price.

b. Even if the Arbitrator Was Not Justified, He Did Not Exceed His Powers

"Unless the contract, the submission, or the rules governing the arbitration provide otherwise, an arbitrator's choice of relief awarded to the prevailing party does not exceed his or her powers so long as it bears a rational relationship to the underlying contract and to the breach thereof as Interpreted, expressly or impliedly, by the arbitrator. This holds true as to any plausible theory of the arbitrator's interpretation of the contract. . . . [T]he existence of an error of law apparent on the face of the award, even one that causes substantial injustice, does not provide grounds for judicial review." (Monroe v. Henson & Bailey.) An award may be vacated only on grounds set forth in CCP §§ 1286.2 and 1286.6. (Id.)

Here, even if the arbitrator made an error in law—which he did not—such an error would not be grounds for judicial review. It is readily apparent that the arbitrator's award of punitive damages bore a "rational relationship to the underlying contract and to the breach thereof." The arbitrator found that the breach was willful, the LRI intended to deceive Riley, and that punitive damages were an "appropriate remedy." Because the parties gave the arbitrator the power to fashion an appropriate remedy, and because it bears a rational relationship to the contract and LRI's willful deception, the punitive damage award must stand. (See Monroe.)

c. Neither CCP §§ 1286.2 Nor 1286.6 Afford LRI Relief From The Proper Determination of Punitive Damages

CCP § 1286.2 lists the various statutory grounds for vacation of an award. These are the only grounds upon which a court may vacate an arbitrator's award. (Monroe.) These grounds include, inter alia, corruption, fraud, undue means, substantial prejudice by misconduct, an arbitrator's exceeding power, and an arbitrator's prejudicial refusal to postpone a hearing for sufficient cause. (See CCP § 1286.2.) LRI has not pleaded that any such circumstances exist in this case. Monroe is clear that an award will not be vacated for reasons outside the statute. Therefore, the decision must stand.

CCP § 1286.6 is equally unhelpful to LRI. It lists grounds for correction of an award by the court. These include, inter alia, the evident miscalculation of figures, the arbitrator's exceeding power, and the correction of the form of the award. (See CCP § 1286.6.) Again, LRI has not pleaded that any of these circumstances are present. Therefore, under Monroe, the court is precluded from correcting the award.

CONCLUSION

Because the arbitrator in this case properly fulfilled his obligations as set forth in the parties' contract and their statement of issues for arbitration, this court should deny LRI's Petition to Vacate.er.

PT-B: SELECTED ANSWER 2

MEMORANDUM IN OPPOSITION OF DEFENDANT'S PETITION TO VACATE
ARBITRATOR'S AMENDED FINAL DECISION AND AWARD

The following constitutes the Plaintiff-Respondent, Riley Instruments, Inc.'s Memorandum in Opposition of the Defendant-Petitioner LRI, Inc.'s Petition to Vacate Arbitrator's Amended Final Decision and Award.

STATEMENT OF FACTS

Riley Instruments, Inc. (Riley) and LRI, Inc (LRI) entered into a contract under which LRI agreed to manufacture and supply computer chips to Riley in accordance with Riley's specification. The contract contained an arbitration provision which required that, "In the event a dispute arises under this contract... the parties agree that the dispute shall be submitted to final and binding arbitration to be conducted under the Manufacturers Arbitration Association (MAA)." The arbitration provision further provided that, "the arbitrator shall award a reasonable attorney's fee to the prevailing party in the dispute." LRI breached its contract with Riley when it consciously decided not to disclose a flaw in the computer chips manufactured for Riley because LRI knew that disclosing such information would cause Riley to reject the chips, as were its rights under the contract. LRI was required under contract to inform Riley on any problems and failed to do so based on this apprehension. The parties submitted the dispute to binding arbitration.

On May 9, 2014 arbitrator Warren issued an initial arbitration award, determining that LRI breached its contract and suffered damages from this breach. The arbitrator found for Riley and awarded contract damages, interest, costs, and administrative fees. The arbitrator found that LRI should take nothing on its counterclaim for recovery of the contract price. However, in this initial award, the arbitrator inadvertently failed to decide several issues submitted by the parties for resolution in the arbitration proceeding. First, the arbitrator failed to determine whether LRI intentionally concealed a manufacturing defect, and if so, what damages Riley should recover as a consequence. Second, the arbitrator failed to decide whether Riley was entitled to punitive damages based on this unconscionable concealment. Finally, the arbitrator failed to award attorney's fees to Riley, the clearly prevailing party in the arbitration. On May 27, 2014 Riley submitted a letter to the arbitrator requesting an amendment of the award to include resolution of these issues and forwarded a copy to opposing counsel. LRI strenuously objected on the unfounded assertion that the arbitrator lacked authority, power, or jurisdiction to amend his award. On May 29, 2014 the arbitrator rendered an amended decision fully resolving all the remaining issues that was favorable to Riley. LRI petitions the court to vacate that final award in the present action.

ARGUMENTS

1. Defendant's Petition to Vacate the Arbitration Award Should Be Denied Because the Arbitrator Had Not Issued a Full and Complete Final Decision Award Based On the Arbitrator's Inadvertent Failure to Render A Decision on All Claims of Merit.

The general rule is that an arbitral decision is not final unless it conclusively decides every point required by and included in the submission of the parties. (Transport). The consequence of an omission to decide all the questions is not addressed in Section 1283 or any other provision of the Columbia arbitration act. (Classic). However, this general rule but be evaluated in light of the common law doctrine of functus officio. (Transport). The doctrine of functus officio means that once the arbitrator has finally decided the submitted issues, their authority over those questions is ended (Transport). However, this common law doctrine has not survived to apply to cases in which an amendment is required to be made of an award that does not address all submitted issues (Classic). The rule of functus officio only survives to bar arbitrators from revisiting and changing complete awards, such as those where the arbitrator in fact decided all the issues presented to them (Classic). However, in the case of incomplete awards, the Columbia Court of Appeals has held that to deny arbitrators the authority to complete their task of deciding all issues does not comport to the public policy behind the

Columbia Arbitration Act and the Supreme Court's instruction that the courts indulge every reasonable intendment to give effect to arbitration proceedings. (Classic). Columbia's contractual arbitration law permits arbitrators to issue an amended award to resolve an issue omitted from the original award through the mistake, inadvertence, or excusable neglect of the arbitrator if the amendment is made before judicial confirmation of the original award, is not inconsistent with other findings on the merits of the controversy, and does not cause demonstrable prejudice to the legitimate interests of any party. (Classic).

In the present arbitration at issue, the arbitrator failed to render a decision on all of the issues presented. First, the arbitrator failed to determine whether or not LRI intentionally concealed a manufacturing flaw. The arbitrator also failed to render a decision based on Riley's argument in their arbitration brief for an award of punitive damages. As such, the arbitrator failed to deal with the issue of concealment, the damages attributable thereto, and the punitive damages remedy. The arbitrator also failed to award attorney's fees as provided for in the arbitration contract. Therefore, as the arbitrator failed to render a final decision that was complete and dispositive of all claims, the arbitrator was permitted to amend his arbitration award to resolve the remaining claims at issue.

2. Defendant's Petition to Vacate the Arbitration Award Should Be Denied Because the Request For Amendment and the Amended Final Decision Award Were Timely Issued Because the Timelines Set Forth in Rule 46 and CCP Section 1284 Do Not Apply to the Arbitration at Issue.

Section 1284 of the Columbia Arbitration Act authorizes an arbitrator, upon written application of a party to the arbitration, to correct the award upon ether of the grounds set forth in Section 1286.6, subdivisions (a) and (c), which provide for correction where there is a miscalculation of amounts, a mistake in the description of a person or property referred to in the award, or where there is a defect in the form of the award that does not affect the merits of the controversy. (Classic). Any application to correct an arbitration award under that section requires notice to the opposing party (Classic). The amendment of an arbitration award resolving the remainder of a dispute does not fall within these subdivisions; therefore the timelines set forth in Section 1284 do not apply. (Classic). Furthermore, the amendment of an arbitration award resolving the remainder of a dispute does not fall within the meaning of "correct[ing] any clerical, typographical, or computational errors in the award," as stated in Rule 46, based on the reasoning set forth in Classic.

In the arbitration at issue, the arbitrator failed to decide all of the issues that were submitted for arbitration. Therefore, he was empowered to amend the arbitration award to resolve the remainder of the dispute between LRI and Riley. As such was an amendment to dispose of all remaining issues and not a correction, the timelines set forth in Section 1284 and Rule 46 do not apply. Based on this reasoning, Riley's request for amendment of the arbitration awards was timely made. Furthermore, Riley provided notice to LRI through forwarding a copy of its request to LRI. Therefore, the court should deny LRI's petition to vacate because the timelines cited by LRI do not apply, rendering the issuance of the amended decision and Riley's initial request for amendment timely.

3. Defendant's Petition to Vacate the Arbitration Award Should Be Denied Because the Arbitrator Was Within the Scope of His Power When He Amended the Decision Award Based on Claims that were Inadvertently Undecided in the Original Award.

Section 1286.2 of the Columbia Arbitration Act sets forth the exclusive grounds for vacating an arbitration award and vacation of an arbitration award may be has if the amended arbitration award was procured by corruption, undue means, or misconduct of the arbitrator. (Classic). It is within the powers of the arbitrator to resolve the entire merits of the controversy submitted by the parties and merits include all the contested issues of law and fact submitted to the arbitrator for decision. (Monroe). Columbia's contractual arbitration law permits arbitrators to issue an amended award to resolve an issue omitted from the original award through the mistake, inadvertence, or excusable neglect of the arbitrator if the amendment is made before judicial confirmation of the original award, is not inconsistent with other findings on the merits of the controversy, and does not cause demonstrable prejudice to the legitimate interests of any party. (Classic).

The arbitrator in the present action admits in the amended decision that he intended, but neglected to, state specifically that LRI intentionally concealed from Riley the manufacturing defect and thereby violated the terms of the contract. The arbitrator also admits that the monetary award included the $75,000 in alleged damages to Riley, but that he failed to itemize the award. The arbitrator also admitted that his failure to address the proposed punitive damages was inadvertent and that he neglected to make a finding on that issue in the initial decision. Finally, the arbitrator admitted that he was required to award attorneys' fees to the prevailing party and that Riley was "obviously" the prevailing party. Therefore, the arbitrator was entitled to make all amendments undertaken based on his inadvertent failure to decide on those submitted issues.

a. The Arbitrator Was Acting Within the Scope of His Powers By Amending the Decision to Decide the Issue of LRI's Intentional Concealment

As stated above, an arbitrator is required to decide all issues submitted to arbitration and is empowered to amend a decision where such an issue has been inadvertently excluded from the decision.

As previously stated, the charge against LRI of intentional concealment was an essential issue to the dispute that was not decided upon in the original decision. While LRI asserts that the arbitrator exceeded the scope of his power by "adding a finding," it was in fact within the scope of the arbitrator's powers to issue a finding on the issue in question. The parties stipulated that this intentional concealment was a relevant issue during the arbitration proceeding. Therefore, the arbitrator was required under the scope of his powers to decide that issue. Based on the arbitrator's inadvertent failure to so decide, the arbitrator acted within the scope of his power to amend the award to include a determination on this claim.

b. The Arbitrator Was Acting Within the Scope of His Powers By Clarifying the Contract Damages Award to Demonstrate How the Final Contract Damages Were Apportioned

There is nothing contained within the MAA Rule nor the Columbia Arbitration Act that prevents an arbitrator from clarifying the apportionment of damages when issuing an amended decision award. The absence of a statutory provision authorizing amendment of an award does not deprive the arbitrator of jurisdiction to do so (Classic).

In the case of the arbitration award at issue, the arbitrator included the award of $75,000 in his total calculation initially. LRI argues in its petition that the arbitrator recharacterized the amount of the contract damages award. However, it was unclear to Riley whether or not the arbitrator failed to award contract damages that would compensate Riley for its damages suffered based on LRI's intentional concealment because the arbitrator did not itemize the contract damages awarded. The arbitrator was within his power to amend the award to provide clarity through itemizing damages that had already been awarded. Therefore, the arbitrator did not exceed his powers.

c. The Arbitrator Was Acting Within the Scope of His Powers By Awarding Attorney's Fees to the Prevailing Party Because He Was Required to do so Pursuant to the Arbitration Clause.

An arbitrator is required to award attorneys' fees to the prevailing party to an arbitration if the arbitration agreement between the parties explicitly states that the arbitrator shall make such an award. An award of attorneys' fees must be determined by the arbitrator, not the court, because it is the arbitrator who is best situated to determine the amount of reasonable attorney' s fees to be awarded for the conduct of the arbitration proceeding. (Marco).

In Marco v. Chandler, the Columbia Court of Appeals held that the arbitrator was required to award attorneys' fees where such a provision controlled the arbitration. The language in the arbitrator agreement in Marco provided that "the prevailing party shall be entitled to reasonable attorneys' fees." This language is less clear than the language present in the LRI-Riley arbitration agreement, which explicitly provides that, "the arbitrator shall award a reasonable attorney's fee to the prevailing party in the dispute." Therefore, the arbitrator was required by the contract provisions to provide a reasonable award of attorneys' fees.

LRI will attempt to argue that because the arbitrator failed to make an explicit finding that Riley the prevailing party, the arbitrator was not required to amend the award to determine the prevailing party and award attorneys' fees. However, it is clear from the face of both the original and amended arbitrator awards that Riley was in fact the prevailing party. In the original award, the arbitrator provided all relief to Riley, absent the relief that was inadvertently omitted from the original award. Furthermore, the arbitrator did not award LRI success on its counterclaim Therefore, it is clear from the terms of both the original award and the amended award that Riley was in fact the prevailing party and as such was entitled to attorneys' fees pursuant to the arbitration agreement.

4. Defendant's Petition to Vacate the Arbitration Award Should be Denied Because the Arbitrator Did Not Commit a Grave Error of Law by Awarding Punitive Damages in a Contract Case Because Errors of Law are Subject to Judicial Review and Arbitrators Are Empowered to Fashion Awards According to What is Just and Good.

The arbitrator may grant any remedy or relief that the arbitrator deems just and equitable and within the scope of the agreement of the parties. (MAA Rule 43). The merits of the controversy between the parties are not subject to judicial review (Monroe). The form and sufficiency of the evidence and the credibility and good faith of the parties, in the absence of corruption, fraud or undue means in obtaining an award, are not matters for judicial review. (Monroe). Arbitrators are not bound by principles of dry law, but may decide on principles of equity and good conscience, and make their award according to what is just and good. (Monroe). In the absence of some limiting clause in the arbitration agreement, the merits of the award, either on questions of fact or of law, may not be reviewed except as provided in the Columbia Arbitration Act (Monroe). Unless the contract, the submission, or the rule governing the arbitration provide otherwise, an arbitrator's choice of relief awarded to the prevailing party does not exceed the scope of his or her powers so long as it bears a rational relationship to the underlying contract and to the breach thereof as interpreted, expressly or impliedly, by the arbitrator. (Monroe). This requires a logical connection. (Monroe). The existence of an error of law apparent on the face of the award, even one that causes substantial injustice, does not provide grounds for judicial review (Monroe).

LRI alleges that the arbitrator erred in awarding punitive damages in a contracts case. While typically punitive damages are available only in specified areas of law, such as tort, an arbitrator is not bound by such technicalities. Here, the arbitrator found that LRI's concealment was intentional and with a motive to deceive. Furthermore, the arbitrator found LRI's conduct unconscionable and found that the intentional breach of contract based on this unconscionability warranted the imposition of punitive damages to punish LRI for its conduct. This imposition of punitive damages is logically connected to the actions undertaken by LRI and is rationally related to the conduct of LRI in breaching the contract. Therefore, the relief of punitive damages awarded by the arbitrator was not made in grave error of law as such a decision is not reviewable by the court and the arbitrator was empowered by both statutory and common law to fashion awards that are just and good. Here, punitive damages as a result of LRI's unconscionable actions would not cause LRI a substantial injustice. Therefore, the award of punitive damages must stand.

CONCLUSION

In conclusion, the court must deny LRI's Petition to Vacate the Arbitration Award for several reasons. First, LRI's Petition to Vacate the Arbitration Award should be denied because the arbitrator had not issued a full and complete Final Decision Award based on the arbitrator's inadvertent failure to render a decision on all claims of merit. As previously stated, the arbitrator failed to render a decision on several key issues submitted by the parties for arbitration. Second, LRI's Petition should be denied because the request for amendment and the Amended Final Decision Award were timely issued because the timelines set forth in Rule 46 and CCP Section 1284 do not apply where there is an arbitration amendment, as they only apply to corrections made to arbitration decision, as defined by common law. Third, LRI's petition should be denied because the arbitrator was acting within the scope of his power when he amended the Decision Award based on claims that were inadvertently undecided in the original award. While LRI contends in its petition that the doctrine of functus officio ended the arbitrator's power to amend the award, this doctrine does not apply to arbitration decision that are not complete, as is the case here. Therefore, the arbitrator acted within the scope of his power to amend the original award to add the finding that LRI intentionally concealed the manufacturing defect, clarifying the damages awarded to demonstrate such a finding, and awarding attorney's fees as he was required to do under the arbitration agreement. Finally, the court should deny LRI's Petition because the arbitrator did not commit a grave error of law by awarding punitive damages in a contract case because errors of law in an arbitration decision are not subject to judicial review and arbitrators are empowered to fashion awards according to what is just and good. On the basis of these forgoing conclusions, the court must deny LRI's Petition to Vacate the Amended Final Decision and Award.

www.ingramcontent.com/pod-product-compliance
Lightning Source LLC
Chambersburg PA
CBHW081732220526
45468CB00008B/2066